#		
64	Mazyck St. at Broad St. 17 Ft. from Queen to Beausain St.	20
65	Short St. 20 Ft. 66 Allen St. at Broad St. 29 Ft. at Queen	32
67	Archdale St. 32 Ft. 68 Magazine St. 20 Ft. 69 West St.	19
70	Boule Alley at Archdale St. 8 Ft. at King St.	7
71	Dutch Church Alley 13 Ft. 72 Beresford St.	25
73	Beautain St. at Mazyck St. 40 Ft. at King St.	31 6
74	Cummins St. Width unknown West side belonging to Harleston not laid out	
75	Saint Philips St.	40
76	Wentworth St. by King St. 46 Ft. by Cummins St.	50
77	Liberty St.	39

Names of the Wharfs

78	Gibbs Wharf	89	Champneys Wharf	
79	Blakes Do	90	Jervey's Do	
80	McKenzies Do	91	Cochrans Do	
81	Ropers Do	92	Prioleaus Do	
82	Eveleighs Do	93	Gillion's Do	
83	Vanderhorsts Do	94	Vanderhorst Do	
84	Guerines Do	95	Shrewsburys Do	
85	Market Dock	96	Munro's Do	
86	Mottes Wharf	97	Mey's Do	
87	Greenwoods Do	98	Laurens Do	
88	Beils Do	99	Gadsdens Do	

NAMES of PUBLIC BUILDINGS

A New Baptist Church
B Old Do Do
C Presbyterian Do
D Guard House
E Treasury, & Auditor Generals Office
F St. Michaels Episcopal Church
G Formerly State House now Court House &c.
H Beef Market
I Low Market
K Exchange
L Fish Market
M French Church
N St. Philips Episcopal Church
O Old Independent Do
P Methodist Do
Q Quaker Do
R New Independent Do
S German Do
T Jews Synagogue
V Distillerys
U Cravens Bastion
W Romish Church
X Brew House

N.B. the Brick Houses colored thus ■
the Wood Do Do ■

35 Public Wells marked thus
9   Fire Engine belonging to the City
N.B. There are private Wells in general throughout the City

CHARLESTON,

Carolina

...unno, Esq. For the use of the

...PANY of LONDON

...y 2d August 1788 by

Edmund Petrie

Privateers in Charleston 1793-1796

AN ACCOUNT OF A FRENCH PALATINATE IN SOUTH CAROLINA

SMITHSONIAN STUDIES IN HISTORY AND TECHNOLOGY
NUMBER 1

Privateers in Charleston

1793–1796

MELVIN H. JACKSON
*Curator of Marine Transportation
National Museum of History and Technology*

SMITHSONIAN INSTITUTION PRESS
CITY OF WASHINGTON
1969

1969 O—294–341
UNITED STATES GOVERNMENT PRINTING OFFICE
WASHINGTON : 1969

For sale by the Superintendent of Documents, U.S. Government Printing Office
Washington, D.C. 20402 - Price $3.50

Foreword

The privateer was a privately owned vessel bearing a commission from a sovereign state that empowered her to seize declared enemies of that state on the high seas. Such seizures, or prizes, after due process in the courts of the sovereign or of friendly powers, became the property of the captor to do with as he would. The license under which the privateer operated was known as a letter of marque and reprisal, and in time the vessel bearing such a commission came to be known as a "Letter of Marque."

All too often the letter of marque was used as a legal cloak for banditry on the high seas, and efforts over the centuries to restrict the worst features of privateering evolved an elaborate body of international convention and domestic regulations. By the early nineteenth century, however, privateering finally came to be recognized for the incorrigible institution it was, and in 1856 it was swept away by the Treaty of Paris, to which, it is interesting to note, the United States and Spain did not subscribe.

Privateering as a form of warfare persisted over so many centuries largely because it was a cheap weapon. For France at the outbreak of the long Wars of the French Revolution—her caste-ridden navy long neglected and destroyed at last by social upheaval—privateering was a weapon of last resort—

but, it must be noted, one for which history records her longtime predilection.

For the investor and the seaman alike, the potent lure of privateering naturally was the quick dollar: "Any Seaman or landmen that have the inclination to make their Fortunes in a few Months May have an opportunity by applying to . . . ." read the broadside nailed to the tavern door. Grateful governments, eager to strike a blow against the wealth-bearing commerce of an enemy, granted letters of marque to all who met a few simple requirements. Inquiries into the character of the outfitters, if made at all, were casual. Bonding, if required to insure compliance with international law, was only casually enforced. Privateering, therefore, tended to attract the unprincipled, and therein lay the evils of the institution that often led its practitioners to the borders, and beyond, of outright piracy.

For the owners, a privateer armed, provisioned, and ready for sea might represent a heavy investment. If they committed their vessel to all-out commerce raiding, the risk to their capital was greater than if the letter of marque was used as an adjunct to normal cargo carrying, during which the seizure of a chance prize might enhance the profits of carriage. The commerce raider, on the other hand, could roam the seas at will, trimmed to her fastest sailing lines, uncluttered with cargo, and carrying a crew large enough to work the ship, handle the guns, and man the prizes she took.

Glorious single-ship actions and bloody resistance were shunned. The aim of the privateer was to capture, not to destroy, enemy shipping, and investors, captain, and crew worked together under the best of incentive plans—No prize, no pay! These men, no matter how highly they were motivated by patriotism, were far more horrified by red ink than by blood. For her part, the merchant ship, deeply laden and difficult to maneuver, and more than likely under-armed and shorthanded, was seldom a match for a determined privateer. The merchant captain, aware of the futility of fighting or running away from such an adversary, often would fire a gun to windward to salve his honor and then haul down his colors. For the most part, the bringing to and surrender of a merchantman, armed or unarmed, was as formalized as a quadrille.

History affords examples of prizes of inordinate value, yet over the years the vast majority of privateers had indifferent

FOREWORD

success. Enemy merchantmen were not easy to find. Often they were under the protection of heavily armed men of war. As a result, a prize once taken was seldom released, even if her papers seemed to be in order. It was too well known that vessels might carry double or even triple sets of papers during times of war, and might sail under as many different flags as did the privateer herself as she worked into hailing distance of a strange sail.

Handling of the prize prior to adjudication of her case ashore varied from punctilious observance of international convention to acts of piracy. The prize's stores or cargo might be pilfered by the privateer crew, her papers might be tampered with or destroyed entirely to insure condemnation, and often her captain and officers were detained, or set ashore in some distant part, to make certain that no libelant would appear before the court to challenge the legality of the capture or to tie up the proceeds of the sale in endless legal red tape.

To walk the thin edge of legality, then, was the everyday lot of the privateer commander. Some fell off. Others, using forged papers and abetted by corrupt port officials, operated as little more than outright pirates—*gens sans aveu*.

The French-commissioned privateers sailing out of Charleston who are the subjects of this study exhibited all of these traits. And the emotional motivation of those who sailed aboard their vessels—the burning anglophobia of French and American alike—was important and accounted for much of the bravura, daring, and scoundrelism that characterizes their story.

This study develops a facet of a larger work in progress on the privateering wars in the Caribbean, 1793–1801. To those who read, corrected, and offered invaluable suggestions regarding it, I wish to express my gratitude: to Robert Greenhalgh Albion, who really started all this; to Dr. Ulane Bonnel, for her guidance in French maritime affairs; to my colleague Howard I. Chapelle, an inexhaustible source of information on the ships and shipping of the eighteenth century; to Donald Green and Terrence Murphy, for eliminating the worst of my outrages against the language of the law; to Peter F. Copeland of the Smithsonian's Office of Exhibits, for his advice and assistance with the illustrations; to Welles Henderson, who graciously supplied photographs of a fine painting in his collection, showing a French privateer overhauling an American ship; to the late John Gaillard Stoney, for conjuring up for me the Charleston of the late eighteenth century; to Virginia Rugheimer, of the Charleston Library Society, for her patient help; to Mary E. Braunagel, for reading the galley proofs; and finally, to my wife Faith Reyher Jackson, who, although weary of privateering, never failed me during the long voyage.

Such errors in fact or judgment that may appear can only be my own.

M.H.J.

February 1969

See End Papers

"*Ichnography of Charleston, South Carolina, At the Request of Adam Tunno, Esq. for the use of the Phoenix Fire-Company of London, Taken from Actual Survey, 2ᵈ August 1788 by Edmund Petrie. Published 1ˢᵗ Jan.ʸ 1790 by E. Petrie N.º 13 America Square." From United States Coast and Geodetic Survey Library Archives.*

See Title Page

"*A view of Charles-Town, the Capital of South Carolina. From an original Picture painted at Charles-Town, in the Year 1771. Published as the Act directs 3ᵈ June 1776, by S. Smith, Green Street, Lavender Fields, London. Painted by Thoˢ. Leitch. Engraved by Samuel Smith." The original painting by Thomas Leech hangs in the Museum of Early Southern Decorative Art, in Winston Salem, North Carolina, and engravings made from it hang in that Museum and in the Gibbes Art Gallery of the Carolina Art Association, Charleston, South Carolina. Reproduction of the engraving on the title page of this work is by courtesy of these Museums.*

Contents

		Page
	INTRODUCTION	1
1	THE PRELUDE TO CHARLESTON PRIVATEERING	3
2	GALLOMANIA AND THE EAST FLORIDA EXPEDITION	21
3	THE WAY IS CLEARED BY THE UNITED STATES DISTRICT COURT	47
4	THE PALATINATE CHALLENGES UNITED STATES NEUTRALITY	63
5	JAY'S TREATY: THE GREAT BETRAYAL	91
6	THE PROFITS OF PRIVATEERING	107
	BIBLIOGRAPHY	111
	APPENDIX	115
	1 Memorial by Jean François Théric, Translated from the Manuscript Original (see Bibliography)	117
	2 British, Spanish, and Dutch Prizes Brought into the Ports of Charleston, South Carolina, and Savannah, Georgia, between April 1793 and April 1796, by French Privateers Based at or Frequenting Those Ports	127
	INDEX	155

LIBERTÉ, ÉGALITÉ.

AU NOM DE LA RÉPUBLIQUE FRANÇAISE.

LE CONSEIL EXÉCUTIF PROVISOIRE DE LA RÉPUBLIQUE FRANÇAISE permet, par les présentes, à   de faire armer et équiper en guerre un nommé le   du port de   tonneaux, ou environ, actuellement au port de   , avec tel nombre de canons, boulets, et telle quantité de poudres, plombs, et autres munitions de guerre et vivres qu'il jugera nécessaire pour le mettre en état de courir sur les pirates, forbans, gens sans aveu, et généralement sur tous les ennemis de la République Française, en quelque lieu qu'il pourra les rencontrer, de les prendre et amener prisonniers avec leurs navires, armes, et autres objets dont ils seront saisis, à la charge, par ledit de se conformer aux Ordonnances de la Marine, aux Lois décrétées par les Représentans du Peuple Français, et notamment à l'article IV de la Loi du 31 Janvier, concernant le nombre d'hommes devant former son équipage, de faire enregistrer les présentes Lettres au Bureau des Classes du lieu de son départ, d'y déposer un rôle, signé et certifié de lui, contenant les noms et surnoms, âge, lieu de naissance et demeure des gens de son équipage, et à son retour, de faire son rapport par-devant l'Officier chargé de l'Administration des lasses, de ce qui se sera passé pendant son Voyage.

Le Conseil Exécutif provisoire requiert tous Peuples, amis et alliés de la République Française, et leurs agens, de donner audit toute assistance, passage et retraite en leurs ports avec sondit vaisseau et les prises qu'il aura pu faire, offrant d'en user de même en pareilles circonstances. Mande et ordonne aux Commandans des Bâtimens de l'Etat, de laisser librement passer ledit   avec son vaisseau et ceux qu'il aura pu prendre sur l'ennemi, et de lui donner secours et assistance.

Ne pourront, les présentes, servir que pour   mois seulement, à compter de la date de leur enregistrement.

En foi de quoi le Conseil Exécutif provisoire de la République a fait signer les présentes Lettres par le Ministre de la Marine, et y a fait apposer le sceau de la République.

Donné à Paris le   jour du mois d   mil sept cent   l'an   de la République Française.

Par le Ministre de la Marine.

Introduction

THE WAR TO CRUSH REVOLUTIONARY FRANCE burst its continental boundaries in January of 1793 and became a worldwide maritime conflict which was to rage almost continuously for more than two decades. On April 22 of that year the United States, asserting its sovereign rights, declared itself neutral in the struggle. Within nine months unfolding events brought forth in the United States a series of executive directives and judicial opinions concerning admiralty jurisdiction and treaty interpretations that swept aside the worst aspects of those "entangling alliances" with France—the Treaty of Amity and Commerce of 1778, the Treaty of Alliance "Eventual and Defensive" of the same year, and the Consular Convention of 1787.

For France, rigorous implementation of this American neutrality policy was tantamount to a *coup de grâce* to her efforts to salvage her position in the West Indies. France's navy was in a state of anarchy and her West Indian colonial establishments were in a state of civil war and political chaos. The one effective

---

This diplomatic pro forma copy of the official French letter of marque in use in the 1790s, shown opposite, is now in the United States National Archives. Very possibly it was delivered to the Department of State by Edmund Genêt upon his arrival at Philadelphia. The French governors of outlying possessions were empowered to issue their own commissions, and when Victor Dupont became consul at Charleston in 1796, he reported that letters of marque were being counterfeited and retailed at that port.

naval weapon remaining to her was the privateer. Since much privateering was carried on in small vessels incapable of keeping the sea for extended periods of time, ports close to traveled trade routes and convenient for repairs and refitting, the refreshment of crews, and disposal of prizes were highly necessary. For France to be closed out of such facilities along the North American coast would be disastrous. France had a foretaste of this between June 1793 and January 1, 1794, when the United States Government took steps systematically to thwart French privateering enterprises in ports north of the Cape Fear River. Had not Charleston, South Carolina, kept its port open to the French raiders during this critical period, 1794 through 1795, the British might have accomplished the total liquidation of the French West Indian empire with unassessable effects on the long war.

The activities of those privateers which used Charleston as their base during the years 1794 and 1795, how they managed to cling to their "forlorn hope," what they accomplished, and the effect of their effort on the war in the Caribbean and on the port which showed them hospitality, is the concern of this study.

Chapter 1

THE PRELUDE
TO
CHARLESTON PRIVATEERING

From the very beginning of the war the French Foreign Office thought of Charleston as a primary base on United States soil. The city was strategically located in relation to Saint Domingue[1] and, to a lesser extent, to the French Windward Islands of the Lesser Antilles. Charleston's position on the flank of the Gulf Stream, the highway of Europe-bound West Indian commerce, made her a logical haven for privateers. No less important was Charleston's proximity to Spain's North American possessions in the Floridas and Louisiana. The revolutionizing of those Provinces was an important part of France's war plans, as is indicated in the original and supplemental instructions issued to that nation's Minister Plenipotentiary to the United States, Edmond Charles Genêt.

Many reasons can be advanced to account for the toleration Charlestonians extended to the French privateersmen long after the northern ports had turned them away. From our vantage point in time the reasons often have a strange perverseness about them.

The historian Ulrich B. Phillips, analyzing the political attitudes of South Carolinians in general, felt that much could be explained by South Carolina's history as a frontier colony. It

---

[1] As that portion, now modern Haiti, of the Island of Hispaniola was called when it was a French colony. The Spanish colony on the island, Santo Domingo, is now the Dominican Republic.

had been, he said, isolated from the main currents of colonial thought that prevailed in older northern colonies and the situation was complicated by "the centralization of commerce, social, and political life by reason of the great importance of the city of Charleston." [2] The feeling of self-sufficiency which such conditions generated, Phillips felt, explained much of the history of South Carolina through the Civil War and after.

This sense of "apartness" was a salient feature of Charleston as a city,[3] for, compared with the cities of the middle and New England states, it had a certain foreignness about it, even something of the exotic. This city—with its fine homes of distinctive architecture, its parks, theatres, and elegant society, in which moved many men and women who traced their French ancestry to the Huguenot emigrees of the 17th century—was notably more European than "Yankee." The luxuriance of its subtropical vegetation, the brilliance of its flowers, the mildness of its winters were more evocative of Saint Domingue's Port au Prince than of Boston, New York, or Philadelphia. As for the rest of the South, there was nothing that could compare with Charleston.

The nature of the southern economy, combined with its geographic and psychic isolation, produced a marked time lag in the resolution of South Carolina's post-Revolutionary-War economic troubles,[4] troubles which had been common to the United States as a whole during the interval between the end of the American Revolution and the outbreak of war between France and England.

---

[2] "South Carolina Federalists, I." *American Historical Review* vol. 14, no. 3 (April 1909), p. 529.

[3] When E. S. Thomas, who later became editor of Charleston's *City Gazette*, arrived there on June 10, 1795, he found the appearance of the city "so totally different from Boston, that I could scarcely realize the idea that it was part of the American Union and under the same government" (*Reminiscences of the Last Sixty-Five Years*, vol. 1, pp. 30–31). An earlier visitor, JOHANN DAVID SCHOEPF, in his *Travels in the Confederation [1783–1784]* (transl. and edit. by Alfred J. Morrison, Philadelphia: William J. Campbell, 1911), noted that "the manners of the inhabitants of Charleston are as different from those of the other North American cities as are the products of their soil . . . . luxury in Carolina has made the greatest advance, and [in] their manner of life, dress, equipage, furniture, everything denotes a higher degree of taste and love of show, and less frugality than in the northern provinces."

[4] At Thomas Jefferson's request, on October 15, 1784, the Charleston Chamber of Commerce forwarded statistics regarding that city's pre- and post-Revolutionary foreign trade. In a comment accompanying the statistics it was noted that "Corn,

1: PRELUDE TO CHARLESTON PRIVATEERING

The attendant social unrest which dominated the period between the Treaty of Paris in 1783 and the adoption of the Constitution of 1787 was alleviated to a great extent in the northern seaboard States with the revival of trade and reforms in State governments. But in South Carolina the effects of the postwar depression were still manifest as late as 1792 and governmental reforms were resisted sharply by the oligarchic clique in control of the legislature. A type of unrest such as Massachusetts had experienced during the Shaysite agitation persisted and became a fertile seedbed for the radical propaganda that increased in virulence as France's period of constitutional monarchy gave way before the onslaught of the Jacobins.

The Charleston radicals blamed the "aristocratical" planter-merchant oligarchy for all the ills suffered by the artisan-mechanic class of the port city and the small upland, non-slave-owning farmer. Such men as Alexander Gillon [5] and Dr. James Fallon had been busy organizing an alliance of the oppressed as early as 1783 [6] and had succeeded in plunging South Carolina into an era of internal strife and bitterness aimed at destroying the power of the oligarchy. The course of the French Revolution provided inspiration and guidelines for their efforts.

Neither the excesses of the Terror nor the decree of February 4, 1794, which emancipated—on paper at least—the slaves of the French colonial population, diminished the admiration of the radicals for the arms of Revolutionary France. Anti-British sentiment had been carefully cultivated by them for years by identifying the ruling oligarchy with the loyalists and crypto-loyalists who had served England's interest during the years of the Revolution. The enormities perpetrated by the British during their occupation of Charleston and their devastation of the

---

Pease, Beef and Pork, and Lumber of all sorts were chiefly shipped to the West Indies, which is not prohibited . . . very little of said articles being shipped to other islands, or at most, not one fifth part of the lumber." This was accompanied by laments about the effects of British trade restrictions and a Portuguese prohibition on rice ("A Journal of the Charleston Chamber of Commerce, commencing 6 of February, 1784").

[5] Commodore Alexander Gillon was a violent anglophobe and the guiding spirit behind the Marine Anti-Britannic Society. Gillon had been commander of various naval forces raised by South Carolina during the Revolution. Lieutenant Governor of South Carolina, 1789–1791, he was elected to Congress in 1793 and maintained a strong anti-British posture until his death in October 1794.

[6] PHILLIPS, "South Carolina Federalist I," pp. 534–537.

countryside was a vivid memory. The failure of French Admiral Charles Hector d'Estaing at Savannah in October 1779 was forgotten. At least the French had come to help their American friends by land and sea. Thus, when Citizen Genêt landed at Charleston, April 8, 1793, on his way to assume duties at Philadelphia as Minister Plenipotentiary, he was feted as a paladin in the great crusade against tyranny and injustice. Indeed, it has been held that the warmth of Charleston's reception of the Minister and its enthusiasm for him went far toward determining his later course of action, which in the end embarrassed France's plans for Franco-American cooperation.

Genêt's stay at Charleston was brief but busy. His first act was to issue letters of marque to hastily organized privateering syndicates. Within ten days of his arrival, the first of five identifiable "Consular Privateers" cleared port to cruise against the enemies of the Republic. Consular prize courts were activated in accordance with France's interpretation of the several Franco-American treaties. Between personal appearances called for by a heavy schedule of celebrations, Genêt met with favorably disposed South Carolina notables, and the expedition against the Spanish Provinces was sketched out for Michel Ange Bernard Mangourit, French consul at Charleston, to develop and mature. Subsequent to Genêt's departure in mid-April for Philadelphia, the first flurry of privateering died down as the raiders forsook Charleston for northern waters, and Mangourit concentrated with exemplary zeal and determination on intrigue and on recruiting for the Spanish adventure.

As Genêt traveled overland toward Philadelphia he was feted enthusiastically all along his route. Manifestations of popular attachment to the French cause undoubtedly had their effect on the Minister as he jolted along, and led him to reevaluate the instructions which were to guide him.

The French National Convention was convinced that existing treaties with the United States provided the necessary legal basis for carrying out France's plan for maritime war in the waters of the West Indies and the United States. Genêt, therefore, in addition to being charged with the task of provisioning the West Indian colonies and negotiating anticipatory payments on the debt owing to France, was carefully instructed to exact stringent observance of articles 17, 21, and 22 of the Treaty of Amity and Commerce of 1778. These articles, it was held, gave special privileges to the ships of war, public and private,

Edmond Charles Gênet, Minister Plenipotentiary of the French Republic to the United States, 1793–1794. Oil on panel by Ezra Ames, ca. 1809–1810. Courtesy of the Albany Institute of History and Art.

of the contracting parties, and clearly forbade the use of their ports to the enemy. France's position was that its treaty rights made British privateering from American ports impossible. Genêt was to insist, therefore, on the exclusion of British privateers and their prizes from American ports.

These treaty rights were deemed so important that the National Convention emphasized in its instructions to Genêt that he was not to press the issue of the guarantees called for by article 2 of the Treaty of Alliance "Eventual and Defensive" of 1778, although in that treaty the United States clearly undertook to guarantee to France the integrity of her West Indian possessions. Instead, Genêt was ordered to promote a closer commercial alliance between the two nations. France, in short, assumed the same posture of guarantor of neutral rights in time of war that she had taken during the Seven Years War and the

War of the American Revolution. For the moment the United States would be cast in the role of a benevolent neutral rather than a cobelligerent. It was conceived that the United States might well prove more of an embarrassment than an asset as an active ally, since she lacked the means not only of challenging British power on the sea lanes but even of protecting her own shores.

If there was room for possible doubt as to the construction France placed on the two treaties of 1778, the Consular Convention of 1787 was regarded as the clinching argument. The interpretation of this document held that special grants of extraterritorial jurisdiction had been accorded French consular officials to complement and strengthen conceivable vagueness in the earlier treaties. At Charleston Genêt had already implemented the provisions of the Convention by setting up the consular prize court. At about the time of Genêt's arrival at Charleston, however, the United States Government at Philadelphia was already pondering means for curtailing the activities of the American-commissioned French privateers. But as late as May 30 it recognized the right of French privateers to dispose of their prizes in American ports upon paying the same duties imposed on regular importations, though it was silent on the functioning of the French consular prize courts.[7]

By June 5, 1793, however, the Federal Government, outraged by Minister Genêt's indiscretions and perhaps by the alarming growth of pro-French agitation as well, yielded to British Minister George Hammond's importunities to place positive restraints on France's privateering efforts. The Government agreed to confiscate and turn back to their British owners those vessels made prize by the American-commissioned French privateers. On July 15 the Government seized the opportunity provided by the notorious *Petite Democrate*[8] affair to lash out

---

[7] Circular letter, Alexander Hamilton to Collectors of Custom, May 30, 1793 (*American State Papers*, vol. 3, p. 339).

[8] *La Petite Démocrate* (ex-*Little Sarah*), a British brig, was captured by the French frigate *l'Embuscade* in April 1793. Bid in by French interests over the bitter protest of George Hammond, she was fitted out as a privateer. Although Citizen Genêt had promised Secretary of State Jefferson that she would not sail, she did so on July 10 and embarked on a career of raiding that distinctly violated American sovereign rights over coastal waters.

The *Petite Démocrate* affair was used by the Administration to discredit Genêt by revoking his exequatur. Jefferson, who had vouched for Genêt's word was so embarrassed by what seemed to be Genêt's treachery that his position in the

1: PRELUDE TO CHARLESTON PRIVATEERING

against both the French privateers and the French Minister. A positive injunction was issued against what were now regarded as illegally commissioned privateers from using American ports under penalty of confiscating their prizes.

But the mere proscription of the privateers did not make them evaporate. Even granting the Government's right to issue such injunctions, the problem of enforcement was enormous. The machinery for searching out and lodging informations against illegal outfits had to be erected; such as existed was new and untried, and, owing to the slowness of communications, inefficient. Hammond lost little time in placing at the disposition of the United States his own efficient intelligence organization— a network of consuls, agents, and informants. He bombarded the Department of State with information on the activities, real and suspected, of French privateer outfitting. In addition, he gratuitously undertook to tutor Secretary of State Jefferson in the niceties of international law—as to exactly what neutrals could, and could not, do. In many instances the tutoring was needed. The Government, under the new constitution, was still unprepared to thread its way through the tangle of problems of international law with which it was suddenly confronted. Even the fundamental question of whether admiralty jurisdiction resided in State or Federal courts had to be resolved.

The British brig *Betsey* provided a case in point. She was captured on May 3 by the Charleston-commissioned French privateer *le Citoyen Genêt*. The British minister at once entered a libel in the Federal Court in Pennsylvania, claiming that the capture was illegal under international law, and petitioned for the restitution of vessel and cargo to her owners. Against the libellant's claim, the respondent entered a plea to jurisdiction, that is, he pled that the court had no jurisdiction over the case in admiralty, and argued that the libelants had only one means of redress—negotiation. Justice Richard Peters of the Federal Court in Pennsylvania found for the respondent. His opinion concluded that the court was without jurisdiction and hence not empowered to inquire into the validity of the commission held by the vessel *le Citoyen Genêt*.

Consternation in Washington's cabinet was great. If the Federal Government did not have the powers of admiralty, how

---

Federalist cabinet was seriously compromised. That Genêt was sincere in his promise and that the sailing of the raider was effected without his complicity is treated in JACKSON "The Consular Privateers," pp. 92–94.

could it, indeed, maintain maritime neutrality, especially in view of the widespread sympathy of State judges and other officials with Genêt's activities?[9] An appeal on the *Betsey* case was pressed by the Government, but until a pronouncement was made on the important issues, it was virtually powerless to enforce its will.

The *Betsey* case was followed shortly by another based on contravention of the presidential neutrality proclamation. Gideon Henfield, who had signed on the Charleston-commissioned *le Citoyen Genêt* as an officer, arrived at Philadelphia as prizemaster of a French prize. He was immediately arrested and bound over for indictment for contravention of the neutrality proclamation, which specifically forbade American citizens from entering the service of a belligerent. Henfield was brought to trial before a special session of the United States Circuit Court for the District of Philadelphia on July 22, 1793. The jury refused to indict, and on July 28 Henfield was set free, amid a great outpouring of public approbation and sympathy for the French cause.[10]

Meanwhile, the President and his cabinet anxiously consulted over the strained situation. On July 18, notwithstanding Hamilton's objections, President Washington decided to petition the Supreme Court through the office of the Department of State for rulings on treaty obligations and international law. On August 8 the Chief Justice and his associates answered the President's request for direction by respectfully declining to render an "extrajudicial" opinion. They based their objections on the constitutional provision of the separation of powers. The executive, they held, was empowered to call only on his cabinet for advice, not the judiciary, and ended by expressing regret if their action might cause the administration any embarrassment.[11]

Three days after the receipt of the Supreme Court's letter, Secretary of the Treasury Alexander Hamilton took the first tentative step to clarify at least some of the perplexities faced by the officers charged with the enforcement of the neutrality proclamation and to provide them with some guidelines. But this Circular Letter to Collectors of Customs, dated August 11,

---

[9] WARREN, *The Supreme Court in United States History*, vol. 1, pp. 105–107.

[10] *American State Trials*, vol. 4 (1915), pp. 615–636.

[11] The original of this letter, dated August 8, 1793, was signed by John Jay, James Iredell, William Patterson, John Blair, and James Wilson (Miscellaneous Letters, U.S. Department of State).

was productive of even greater confusion.[12] It contained the curious provision that "Equipments of any vessels of France in the ports of the United States which are *doubtful* in their nature as being applicable to commerce or warfare are deemed lawful [italics supplied]."

It is tempting to read into this phrase a certain desire to offset the political and diplomatic repercussions that were expected to follow the Government's action in revoking Genêt's exequatur and to silence some of the bitter allegations of subservience to British interests by the Government's opposition. Article 5 of the Circular Letter specifically refers to the French privateers and in giving great latitude to the judgment of local law enforcement officials it might easily have been construed as reflecting second thoughts on the effect of the Administration's policy on treaty obligations. A privateering entrepreneur taking into account the previous Government dictum might almost feel that he was being directed toward acceptable methods of arming and equipping privateers in United States ports.

Indeed, in the heyday of French privateering out of Charleston, between January 1794 and the end of 1795, subjective interpretations by State officials and local customs officers provided an indispensable *laissez-aller* for the French raiders.

The effectiveness of the Circular Letter of August 11 was put to the test a few days after its issuance, when the British Minister lodged an information against the French armed schooner *l'Industrie*, reported as then lying at Baltimore. In the absence of the Governor of Maryland, some time was lost in rounding up a quorum of the State Council to get the investigation under way. Finally, a man named Kelty was chosen, but Kelty apparently had little taste for the job entrusted to him. After several vain attempts to locate the schooner—which lay in plain sight off Fell's Wharf—Kelty with manifest reluctance placed the vessel in detention.

The owner-master of the schooner *l'Industrie*, Jean Baptiste Carvin, who later became one of the most successful privateer commanders and outfitters based at Charleston, immediately

---

[12] It is interesting to note that 14 months after the date of this circular letter the Treasury Department was forced to elaborate for the benefit of law enforcement officers by use of italic and citing specific examples what was meant by "Equipments, etc." (see Circular Letter to Collectors of the Custom, Treasury Department, October 6, 1794, *American State Papers*, vol. 3, pp. 339–340).

The vessels in this contemporary view of New York harbor are those of Vice-Admiral Sercey's squadron prior to its departure in 1794 (see footnote 16, p. 14). In the left foreground is either l'Eole *or* le Jupiter—*with an American shield and eagle on her head! The frigate is* la Concorde. *The brig and schooner are possibly two of the "proscribed" privateers—the former the notorious* la Petite Democrate (ex-Little Sarah), *her name changed to* la Cornelia, *and the latter her consort* la Carmagnole. *Painting, by Archibald Robertson, in the collection of the National Maritime Museum, Greenwich, England. Courtesy of the Trustees, National Maritime Museum.*

clamored for the return of his vessel. Aided by Citizen Moissonier, French consul at Baltimore, Carvin presented documentary proof that he held a valid commission from the French colonial government at Saint Domingue.

The nature of Carvin's commission was a curious one but it was not questioned. He referred to it as a "license for cruising" by which his vessel was in effect under charter to the colonial government. Under this arrangement Carvin relinquished all prizes to his government and contented himself with a "reasonable gratification." By this agreement it would be difficult to determine whether *l'Industrie* was a Letter of Marque or a public vessel or merely an armed merchantman within the meaning of international convention. In answer to the information that *l'Industrie* had augmented her armament while at Baltimore, Carvin presented further proof that clearly established that his vessel had mounted 16 guns ever since she sailed from Cap Français on April 11, 1793, laden with refugees from the civil war.

Kelty, provided only with Hamilton's equivocal Circular Letter, had a difficult decision to make. From the evidence available to him there could be little doubt that *l'Industrie* at the time of the inquest was qualitatively much better armed than when she entered at Baltimore. Much work had been done to her hull, fittings, and armament. It could not be proved, however, that her armament had been quantitatively increased. The fact of being armed was not conclusive evidence of the belligerent character of a particular vessel, for this was an era in which owners determined whether their vessels would be armed according to the nature of the trade in which they were engaged.[13] Presumptive evidence of the character of the schooner's employment was certainly offered by the abnormal size of her crew but that was evidently not considered conclusive enough to warrant detention.

Kelty's decision to release the French schooner was probably justified in view of the vagueness of the standards afforded him by article 5. But the fact remained that the chief occupation of *l'Industrie* was indeed privateering.[14]

Carvin sailed shortly after the release of his vessel and thumbed his nose at British Minister Hammond by seizing the British ship *Roehampton* off the Virginia Capes. He ordered the prize for Baltimore either under the impression that his status had been fully vindicated or, possibly, out of pure impudence. What he was unaware of as he sailed south was that the Government had rejected Kelty's findings; when the *Roehampton* arrived in port she was promptly seized under the President's directive of June 5 and returned to her owners. Thus, by extension, *l'Industrie* was placed in the category of the "proscribed privateers,"[15] and, as increasing pressure was brought to bear against the activities of the American-commissioned French privateers, one after the other, by September

---

[13] Jefferson, smarting under the harassment of Hammond, who accused him of countenancing French privateering activities in the United States, sought to draw a line between vessels armed for attack (privateers) and merchant ships defensively armed. "Just because she has guns for self protection it does not make her a privateer . . . . Does a husbandman following his plough in time of war become a soldier because he carries a pistol or a knife in his pocket?" (*American State Papers*, vol. 1, p. 68.) In 1794 the U.S. Government attempted to regulate the arming of merchant vessels in order to obtain a measure of control over the export of arms and armed vessels. It did not meet with notable success. (See below p. 68.)

[14] Details of depositions and the investigation of *l'Industrie*'s detention are contained in *British Counter Case and Papers* . . . (hereafter cited as BCC), p. 544.

[15] On the *Roehampton* affair see Jefferson Manuscripts, Jefferson to Bournonville, October 3, 1793; and Miscellaneous Letters, U.S. Department of State, Thornton to Governor Lee of Maryland, October 13, 1793, demanding the arrest of the *Roehampton* and lodging a complaint against *l'Industrie*.

1793, they had disappeared. Some departed for the West Indies, the others were either captured or dismantled or bought up by the French squadron lying at New York.[16]

Other French raiders with impeccable credentials fresh from France came in their place, however, and the problem of neutrality enforcement persisted, awaiting a clear definition of treaty obligations and the admiralty jurisdiction of the Federal Courts. It was not until January 1794 that these problems were resolved. Until then, French privateers continued to bring in their prizes and to dispose of them through their consular courts along the length of the United States coast, at the same time generally flouting Government directives against refitting and recruiting.[17]

As long as French raiding could be carried out with profit and relative impunity in northern waters, Charleston remained only a privateering backwater. Although the most successful of the Charleston-based privateersmen, Jean Bouteille, had brought his schooner *la Sans Pareille* into port for the first time on July 18, 1793, it was not until six months later that Charleston began to assume major proportions as a haven for French privateers.

Bouteille's career paced the rise of Charleston as a raiders' haven. He can be identified as either owning or sharing in at least sixteen privateers by the middle of 1795, and probably he had interests in others. Only Jean Baptiste Carvin could equal him in his achievements at sea. Bouteille, a native of Narbonne in his middle fifties, had come out to Saint Domingue fifteen years earlier to engage in the coasting trade. On the very day that news arrived of the war with England, Bouteille purchased the schooner which he named *la Sans Pareille*, scraped up what

---

[16] This was the squadron which in the summer of 1793 escorted the convoy of refugees from Cap-Français (Cap-Haïtien) to New York and other Atlantic ports as a result of the burning of Le Cap during the civil war that for the previous three years had been devastating the great colony of Saint Domingue. Actually, by November 1793 the fleet, torn by mutiny and political dissension and by revolutionary and counter-revolutionary intrigue, had been dispersed on various fruitless missions and its potential had been frittered away.

[17] As testimony to the smooth functioning of French consular prize courts as late as September 1793, we have the advertisement carried by the Boston *Centinel* (September 9) headed "Consulat de la République Française" soliciting all claims against the Dutch prize *Yonge Gerard* and the British vessels *Harpooner* and *Britain*. In Savannah, the French consulate called for claims against the British ship *Grenada Packet* as late as April 1794 (*Georgia Gazette*, April 24, 1794).

1: PRELUDE TO CHARLESTON PRIVATEERING

armament he could, and obtained a commission from the authorities at Saint Domingue to cruise against the British.[18]

Indications are that he had in mind making for the hunting grounds which lay between the Virginia Capes and Boston for he bypassed Charleston on his way north. En route, off the north coast of Cuba, he made a daring capture of a large and well manned Spanish vessel, *la Santa Catalina,* described as a "flat-bottomed barge."[19] Bouteille took three other prizes, two of which he dismissed after removing their supplies. The third was the Jamaican brig *Betsey,* laden with 35 puncheons of rum, a crew of eight, and one passenger.

On June 22 he brought *Betsey* into Wilmington, North Carolina,[20] but his stay was short. It is not quite clear what happened at Wilmington. There is a confused account of a contretemps involving *Betsey*'s captain, who managed to escape ashore and alerted the authorities to some irregularity in the capture of his vessel, for when *la Sans Pareille* sailed, toward the end of June, it was without the company of his prize.[21] Another factor in Bouteille's abrupt departure might have been the sight of the dismantled, Charleston-commissioned *le Vainqueur de la Bastille,* which had been seized and detained under

---

[18] Information on the background of Bouteille as well as other privateer commanders who operated out of Charleston from mid-1793 to April 1795 is contained in a report from "Jean François Théric, négociant a Charlestown [sic] . . . au Ministre de la marine et des Colonies," "5 frimaire, l'an 4 (26 9bre 1795)." (Hereafter cited as Théric, Memorial.) Théric was active as a privateer agent, and in the spring of 1795 was sent as a deputy of the privateersmen to the National Convention at Paris in order to bring to the attention of France the services of the Charleston-based privateers to the cause. Théric sought recognition for the corsair captains by recommending that certain of them be granted brevet ranks in the French navy. As part of his argument Théric included in his memorial a list of prizes, British, Spanish and Dutch, brought into Charleston as well as a list of privateers regularly operating out of that port. As a gauge of the damage done to enemy commerce he also drew up a balance sheet valuation of the prizes brought in. These are translated in the Appendix, pp. 117–126.

[19] Bouteille's description of *la Santa Catalina* (*American Daily Advertiser,* August 1, 1794) strongly suggests a New Orleans origin, and very possibly she was one of those vessels built and freighted by Americans on the Ohio River, with the east coast of the United States as a destination. Because of Spanish control of the mouth of the Mississippi, such vessels were required, to be cleared for the sea-leg of the journey, to take out Spanish registry and to carry a Spanish master and crew. Bouteille's account further mentions her as under charter to the King of Spain, and although she was pierced for 20 guns, she was unarmed except for 4 cannon in the hold. *La Santa Catalina* was sent to Norfolk, but nothing further on the vessel is ascertainable.

[20] *American Daily Advertiser,* July 12, 1793.

[21] Ibid.

the directive of June 5.[22] This may well have provided Captain Bouteille with an insight into the bleak future of privateering in northern waters and caused him to head south after leaving Cape Fear River.[23]

Bouteille, after first touching at Savannah, brought *la Sans Pareille* into Charleston on July 18 and from that date until 1796 he made that port the base of his operations. For the remainder of 1793 his success was rather indifferent [24] until, toward the end of August, he joined forces with Jean Baptiste Carvin. It seems likely that the two vessels met at sea, while Carvin was en route south from his brush with the Baltimore

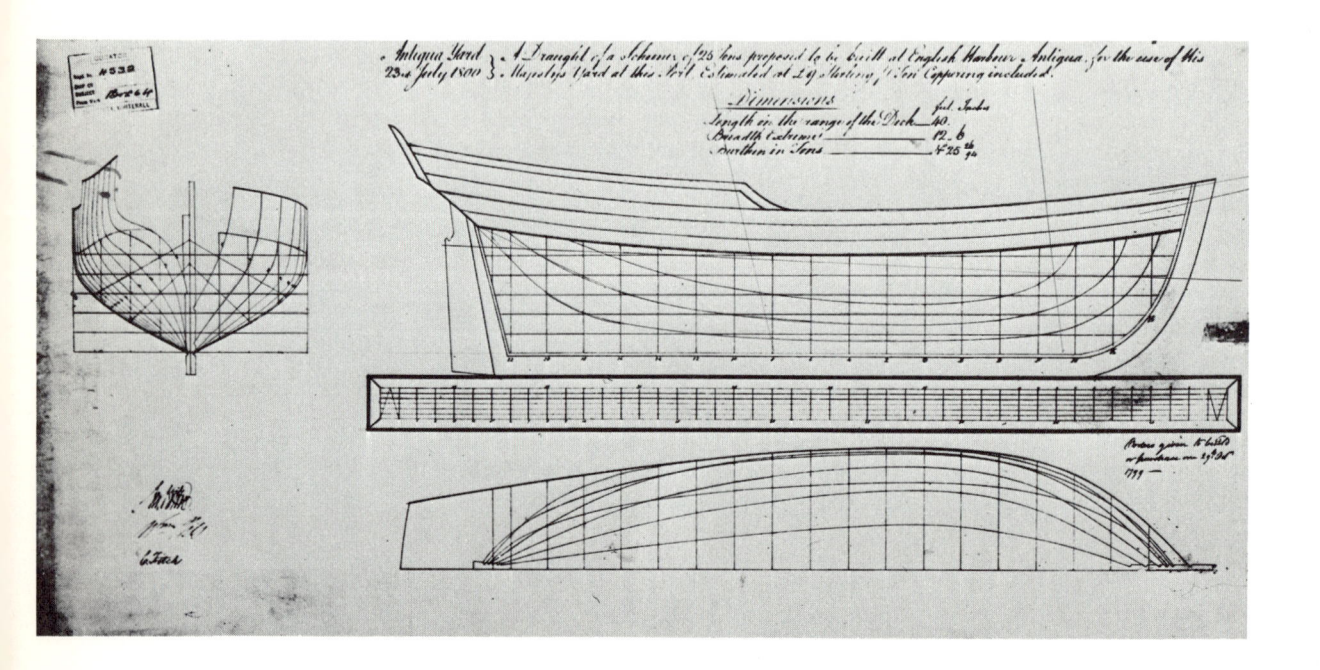

"Draught of a Schooner of 25 tons proposed to be built at English Harbour Antigua . . . 23rd July 1800." Its length along the deck was 40 feet and its extreme beam was 12 feet 6 inches. Small vessels of this type were favorites of the West India privateersmen. With lines reminiscent of the Norfolk pilot boat, they were fast and weatherly. Jean Bouteille's little Sans Pareille *very probably resembled such a vessel.*

[22] BEE, *Reports*, p. 68, *Williamson* v. *Brig Betsey & J. P. Sargeant.*

[23] Two months later Captain Hervieux, another French privateersman associated with Charleston, and captain of several of Bouteille's other privateers, also remarked on the coolness of the Wilmington authorities.

[24] *La Sans Pareille* captured the Hamburg brig *Anna Magdalena* on July 22, having followed her out of port. This vessel was released by the consular prize court on the grounds of Hamburg's neutrality. (*American Daily Advertiser*, August 7, 1793). She also captured the British brig *Jessie*, which proved a profitable prize. Bound for Baltimore from Havana, she carried a cargo listed as 152 casks of molasses, 24 boxes of sugar, 30 hides, 529 dollars in cash, and two bills of exchange, the whole valued at $12,000. (*State Gazette of South-Carolina*, July 29, 1793, and *American Daily Advertiser*, August 10, 1793.) Théric (Memorial, f. 215) gives the value of *Jessie* as £2,015/19/11. She is not mentioned in the Annexes to BCC, listing vessels taken by French privateers from Charleston.

1 : PRELUDE TO CHARLESTON PRIVATEERING

authorities and the capture of *Roehampton* and was doubtless not eager to return northward. A partnership, not uncommon among privateersmen, was struck up between the two captains. The two schooners, the lightly armed *la Sans Pareille* carrying only four swivels and a full crew of 37 men and the heavier *l'Industrie* carrying 16 guns, would have complemented each other well. If her size seems hardly to have merited *la Sans Pareille* a share-for-share arrangement, the skill and daring shown by Bouteille in the capture of *la Santa Catalina,* as noted above, made up for the lack of weight of his small schooner.

The *Sans Pareille-Industrie* partnership produced four joint prizes which arrived at Charleston between September 12 and 25.[25] Thereafter, to the end of 1793 both vessels cruised on their own account with only modest returns.[26]

At the beginning of 1794 Bouteille and Carvin were the only two French privateer captains regularly based at Charleston. Other French privateers certainly called in, but the shipping columns of local newspapers ignored the movements of armed vessels into and out of the port unless they were accompanied by a prize of note. The auction sale notices inserted in the newspapers—a lively indicator of privateering activity—are similarly infrequent until February 1794.

But the lull was a short one. The law courts in the northern States and British naval power in the West Indies were creating pressures that would shortly have great influence on Charleston's development as a French privateering palatinate.

---

[25] These were the following:

Vessel	Stated value (£) BCC	Théric	Sale price (£)
Bark *Two Brothers*	1,669 1 4	1,000	550
Ship *Harriet* (referred to as *Henrietta*)	5,769 19 6	2,000	2,000
Ship *Sovereign*	7,731 10 0	2,210 10 6	500
Snow *Adventure*	1,200 0 0	280	

[26] *La Sans Pareille* captured the British brigs *Maria* and *Argo*, which entered Charleston on October 3 (*New York Journal and Patriotic Register*, October 16, 1793). Although *Maria* is mentioned neither in the Annexes to BCC nor in Théric, these valued *Argo* at £233/6/8 and £280, respectively.

L'Industrie captured the 500-ton ship *Reddington* and ordered her for Norfolk (*New York Journal and Patriotic Register*, October 16, 1793). Since she is not mentioned in either of the above sources, it is presumed that she was retaken. Another vessel, *Aurora* entered Charleston as a prize on December 30, was run through the

It was in Boston, stronghold of Federalism, that the first major blow was struck in behalf of the United States Government against French treaty-right pretentions—in the 1793 decision of the Massachusetts District Court, in the case of *Folger* v. *Lecuyer*.[27]

The case revolved about the capture of the British registered whaler *Harpooner,* Captain Brown Folger, by the French privateer *La Marseille* of Havre de Grâce [Le Havre], commanded by Jacques Louis Lecuyer. Brown Folger, an American citizen, sought to extricate his share from sale of the whaler's cargo, a sale that had been hustled through the consular court at Boston.[28] In his libel Folger based his claim on the fact that the lading of the whaler was made prior to the outbreak of war between France and England, and, in addition, as an American citizen, he cited article 14 of the Treaty of Amity and Commerce between France and the United States, which stipulated that such cargoes were to be exempt from seizure. Lecuyer for his part confidently entered the tried and true "plea to jurisdiction."

On December 6, 1793, the court handed down its decision upholding the jurisdiction of the Federal Courts in cases of admiralty and laid the axe to extraterritorial rights of jurisdiction which the French insisted was the intent of the Franco-American consular convention.

In his rejection of the respondent's claim to such a right, Justice Lowell voiced the clear intent of the Government to extricate the Nation from its embarrassing obligations under the Treaty of Alliance of 1778 in words that were not lost on interested parties:

French consular court, and put up at auction, where she was bought in by Penman & Co. for £150 on behalf of her former master, Captain Dickie, even though the value of the vessel had been set at £4,000 by the British consul at Charleston. Dickie managed to slip out for New Providence, only to fall into Bouteille's hands again two months later. *Aurora* was again put on the block, sold to a man named Smith who cleared her for Boston. (BCC, Annex 1, p. 616). Théric listed her as bringing £1,053/11/0 at her first sale and £3,838/18/9 at the second sale. These figures undoubtedly reflect the gross proceeds of cargo and vessel.

[27] The case papers of *Folger* v. *Lecuyer* and the related docket books are contained in Massachusetts District Court Records, 1788–1799. Lowell's decision was printed in full by the Boston *Centinel*, January 4, 1794.

[28] The Boston *Centinel*, September 9, 1793, carried an advertisement headed "Consulat de la Republique Francaise" soliciting all claims against the Dutch Prize *Yonge Gerard*, and the British vessels *Harpooner* and *Britain*.

It does not appear by the Treaty that it was the contemplation of the contracting parties to make common cause in all future wars in which either of them might be engaged.[29]

Within two months of *Folger* v. *Lecuyer,* Lowells' decision was amplified and settled with finality by the Supreme Court in the case of *Glass* v. *the Sloop Betsey.*[30] This blow to France's maritime strategy of fighting a privateer war in the western hemisphere would have been severe even without reference to her desperate military posture in the Caribbean; compounded with the reverses which had begun to accumulate there in September 1793, it spelled disaster.

From the beginning of hostilities between Great Britain and France, Whitehall had adopted a policy of conquest by intrigue and was content to watch and wait while Saint Domingue dissolved in civil war and the other French islands lapsed into political anarchy. French émigré planters and royalists flocked to both London and to Kingston, Jamaica, seeking British help in ousting the revolutionary governments in return for the restoration of the old regime under British protectorates. British colonial privateers were carrying the main burden of the war in the Caribbean so that the Royal Navy could be husbanded for the indispensable blockade of France's European ports.

In September 1793, however, the war in the Caribbean came to life with the launching of a British amphibious attack against Saint Domingue. That wretched colony, devastated by two years of terrible civil war and stripped of its naval defense, could offer little resistance to the British onslaught. The town of Jérémie was the first to fall, her defenses handed over by a deputation of planters. Three days later the "Gibraltar of the Antilles," Fort Saint Nicholas Mole, capitulated without a shot fired in its defense, and at the end of 1793, by straining available military reserves to the breaking point, Britain had extended her holdings. In the Bight of Leogane, the surrender of Saint Marc and Gonaïves was followed by that of Les Verettes and Petite Rivière; in the south Jean Rabel fell and finally Leogane, Jacmel, and Saltrou. When Mirebelais offered to surrender at the beginning of 1794 the British had to refuse it. Men for garrisoning the town were completely lacking. Subjugation of the entire colony, however, was a foregone conclusion.

---

[29] Massachusetts District Court Records, vol. 1, p. 89.
[30] The case is recorded in Dallas, *Reports.* It is legally cited as 3 Dallas 6(1794).

The British landings on Saint Domingue proved only the prelude to the systematic reduction of remaining French strongholds in the Caribbean. Tobago was captured in February 1794, and soon thereafter Martinique and Saint Lucia, by forces under the command of Admiral John Jervis and General Sir Charles Grey.

By the end of May 1794 France was dispossessed from the Lesser Antilles with the capture of Guadeloupe, while at Saint Domingue a British *coup de grâce* was being readied for the few remaining pockets of French resistance that survived a Spanish invasion from Santo Domingo that captured Fort Dauphin [31] and drove into the central plains. The sole colonial possession wholly in the hands of France in the vicinity of the Caribbean was Cayenne, hedged in by Dutch, Spanish, and Portuguese possessions in alliance with Great Britain.

---

[31] Fort Dauphin lay close to the long disputed boundary between the Spanish and French parts of Hispaniola's north coast. This effort marked Spain's only military adventure in 13 years of Caribbean warfare, during which time she was involved first on the side of the British and later on that of France.

Chapter 2

GALLOMANIA
AND THE
EAST FLORIDA EXPEDITION

AFTER MINISTER GENÊT DEPARTED FOR PHILADELPHIA in mid-April 1793, it was vice-consul Mangourit who took over the promotion of France's grand design to revolutionize and seize from Spain the Floridas and Louisiana.

Seemingly it would have been difficult to find a man with better credentials for the job. As a veteran of the storming of the Bastille and former editor of the Parisian revolutionary newspaper *Héraut de la Nation,* he was the very embodiment of the French Revolution. Since late summer of 1792 he had been assiduously propagandizing Charleston. He encouraged the organization of, and participated in, binational patriotic societies which not only were dedicated to furthering French Republican principles but also were active in soliciting gifts of money and goods for the cause of revolutionary France.

When war broke out between France and England, Mangourit lost little opportunity of reminding Charlestonians of the bestiality of "perfidious Albion." Many French refugees were resident in Charleston. Their experiences at the hands of the British colonial privateers could be heard at first hand, while Peter Freneau kept the columns of his pro-French *City Gazette* liberally sprinkled with extracts from such newspapers as Philadelphia's *American Daily Advertiser* relating the savage attacks of the British "harpies" on the misery-laden refugee fleet from Cap Français. Tales of pilferage, kidnapping, larceny petit and grand, slave snatching, and outrages to womanhood created a widespread revulsion against Great Britain, even in Federalist ranks. That many of the attacks were perpetrated on neutral American vessels engaged in nothing more nefarious than aiding fellow humans in distress served to compound American bitterness.

Under Mangourit's experienced direction, French agents cleverly manipulated American sympathies through the fronts offered by the radical clubs he had carefully nurtured. Thus in August 1793 the Republican Society of Charleston, convinced that the Federal authorities were being dilatory in stopping the arming of the Jamaican merchant sloop *Advice,* assumed the role of the defender of United States neutrality and appointed a committee to demand that the sloop's master land his vessel's guns and ammunitions. Captain Marshall refused. This refusal the committee conveyed to the Society, which determined that in view of Government apathy private action was indicated.

New demands were made. Marshall again refused, saying that only force would make him yield his armament. Another retreat, another meeting, another demand. This last demand, backed by "Captain Cunnington's troops and a batallion of artillery in their uniforms," won the day.[1]

In a letter published in the *State Gazette* on August 12, Captain Marshall sought to explain his conduct in the hope that—

. . . it may tend to soften and not by any means to extend the disgust, which appears unfortunately to have taken place in some instances, I hope unintentionally, between the citizens of America and my fellow citizens.

Diplomatically, he took the opportunity to remind Charlestonians that if international law—which prevented the sailing of belligerent armed vessels within 24 hours of an enemy—had been observed by the American authorities, he "never should have had an idea of arming."[2]

Nevertheless, popular enthusiasm was kept at a high pitch by carefully organized demonstrations on the occasion of the news of France's field triumphs in Europe. The victories of Dumouriez in the Low Countries were the occasion of a two-day gala

---

[1] The patriots triumphantly relieved *Advice* of 3 6-pounders (double fortified), 2 3-pounders, 4 swivels, 325 rounds of shot, some grape, and a number of pistol balls. Further detective work turned up 3 unfinished gun carriages in a blacksmith shop as well as some 70 men who, purportedly, were prepared to join the sloop after she had crossed the bar. (*State Gazette of South-Carolina,* August 9, 1793.)

[2] Ibid., August 12, 1793. Marshall's letter is headed "on board the cutter *Advice* of Jamaica . . .," whereas the account of August 9 refers to the sloop *Active.*

in January 1794 that was minutely chronicled in the press.[3] In February 1794 the Republican Society of Charleston, much frequented by Mangourit, celebrated another such victory, and the splendid civic feast it occasioned was duly noted by the public press as far away as Philadelphia.

At 2 p.m. of the gala day the members of the Society, with their special guest, the consul general of the French Republic, assembled at Citizen Harris' hotel. From there the Society, the members' hats decorated with the French national cockade, and bearing branches of laurel surmounted by liberty caps, proceeded to City Hall where an oration was delivered by that dedicated Francophile Stephen Drayton. As a recessional the members returned to Harris' Hotel in the same order that they went, with drums beating and fifes tootling *Ça Ira,* to partake of an elegant collation.

Charleston's population, already enlarged by refugees from Saint Domingue, was further swelled by an influx of soldiers of

---

[3] Ibid., January 17, 1794.

Transfer-printed Liverpool-type cream-ware pitchers, ca. 1792–1795. McCauley Collection, in the Smithsonian's National Museum of History and Technology.

fortune and seafarers scenting booty and prize money. Swaggering filibusterers and privateersmen of every maritime nation of Europe and America elbowed citizens off Charleston's narrow sidewalks. Drunken, raucous, and riotous, they filled the boardinghouses, taverns, and theatres to overflowing. They tendered public banquets at which, according to the custom of the day, they orated and they drank innumerable toasts to the brotherhood of the two republics and confusion to Pitt and the British slaves.[4] By the end of 1793 the hooliganism in the streets of Charleston offered an opportunity for an ironic comment on the spread of "gallomania:"

> It has been an old adage that the people of the French nation were the most accomplished and polite in the world. But, I am sorry to see the proverb so extremely reversed by the behaviour of most of them in this city. Having generally the occasion to pass the corner of Queen-street and the Bay, two or three times a day, and frequently through the Dirty Street, while a crowd of from ten to thirty heroes, of the *pistol, dagger* and *sword,* keep full possession of the pavement, not even giving way to ladies! It was Saturday last, two gentlemen had the hardiness to break in upon their ranks (one a member of the Republican society) when they had like to have suffered for their presumption in brushing past those sons of thunder; for they were immediately accosted with *Sacra Bougra,* etc., etc., etc., and were actually pursued to be revenged for the insult, until they took sanctuary in a store adjoining. How far this menacing our civil citizens walking in the open day can be remedied, time will develop.
>
> A CITIZEN [5]

It was during this period that Jean Bouteille began to cut the figure for which he was so long remembered. With the proverbial prodigality of the seafarer ashore Bouteille vied with the societies in glorifying the feats of the armies of the Republic. Not only did he proffer and pay for out of his own pocket lavish civic feasts, attended by Charleston's leading figures, but in the manner of an Arabian prince he distributed gifts of bread, food, and money to the poor. At one banquet Bouteille placed a gold guinea under the plate of each of his guests. At another, as though to avoid a repetition of such vulgar ostentation, theatre tickets were substituted.[6]

---

[4] FRASER, *Reminiscences of Charleston*, p. 39.
[5] *Columbian Herald,* December 12, 1793.
[6] FRASER, *Reminiscences*, pp. 12, 34-46. Writing more than a half century later, Fraser gives a vivid account of the ebullient period of French privateering out of Charleston. Ebenezer Thomas, who came to Charleston a year after Bouteille's more extravagant entertainments, 40 years later remembered that people were

As adroitly as Mangourit managed his propaganda campaign did he set about the main business at hand—putting into execution the French Republic's "grand design" against the two Spanish Floridas and Louisiana. Under the benign patronage of Governor Moultrie, Commodore Gillon, Stephen Drayton, and others, the dissidents and ambitious of South Carolina and Georgia were drawn into the conspiracy. To handle the raising of Indian allies among the Creeks, Mangourit had the aid of the brothers William and Samuel Hammond, ably assisted by another brother, Abner, partner in Hammond and Fowler, an American firm with business ambitions in Spanish Florida. Even George Rogers Clark of Revolutionary War fame was not adverse to considering the possibilities presented by the destruction of Spanish power in North America. Recruiting was pressed. Soon the "Revolutionary Legion of Florida" took shape. For his part, Mangourit maintained the fiction of respecting United States neutrality. He asserted that recruiting for the Florida Legion was carried out beyond the borders of the country, but it was patent that Charleston was the general headquarters for the expedition, and houses of rendezvous were operated quite openly in the city.

The vexations of organization were endless. For every needed article—from arms and ammunition to needles and thread—the Charleston merchants had run up the price to such an exorbitant amount that Mangourit was forced to seek military essentials through Genêt and as far afield as New York and Philadelphia. Capable leaders had to be attracted, their vanity fed, and their cupidity assuaged. The good will and cooperation of the Creeks and Cherokees had to be insured with gifts of cocked hats, French uniforms, cockades, handkerchiefs, toys, mirrors, razors, scissors, knives, hatchets, and a thousand and one other items. Treaties had to be prepared, proclamations issued, and agents sent out to report back on the state of public opinion in New Orleans and on the constitution of the garrison and armament at Saint Augustine. Officials in Georgia and

---

still talking about them when he arrived there. (THOMAS, *Reminiscences*, vol. 1, p. 32.) Théric (Memorial, f. 212 v.), in seeking recognition of Bouteille's privateering feats from the Directory, recounted Bouteille's generosity to the poor, and said that by Germinal (April) 1795, when Bouteille's privateering interests encompassed no fewer than 38 vessels he negotiated with a Spanish commissioner the exchange of some 30 French seamen held captive in Havana for a new vessel of 350 tons, also from his own pocket. (*City Gazette*, April 6, 1795: "Saturday arrived brig *John and Phillip*, Bourden, Havana with 200 [sic] French prisoners on board.")

South Carolina had to be seduced, placated, flattered, or otherwise rendered sympathetic. But since Mangourit was almost entirely dependent on Genêt for supplies, money, and a naval covering force to guarantee the success of the projected attack, he grew alarmed, by the Minister's delays and evasiveness. By the end of December 1793, it became clear that Genêt, burdened with mutinous French naval units at New York and embroiled in partisan feuding with the French refugees and in his quixotic campaign to topple President Washington's unfriendly Federalist Administration, would never be able to produce the needed elements.

Slowly it became clear to Mangourit that the ascendancy of French sympathies in the United States would not override the determination of the Government to eliminate any possible compromise with the maintenance of strict neutrality. The fateful issue of French treaty rights was already in the northern courts when Mangourit decided that it was imperative to prepare a stronghold from which the war at sea could be carried on against the enemies of the Republic. As a consequence, the original design for conquest of a vast area was scaled down to East Florida, with Amelia Island on the Saint Marys River as the immediate beachhead to be seized. This port would at least serve as a stronghold for the French privateers in the event that French privileges in United States ports should be abrogated. There, just south of the boundary that divided the United States from East Florida, a thriving entrepôt could be set up.

In a memoir published in Paris in 1795, after he had been recalled to answer for his administration of French affairs at Charleston, Mangourit set forth the rationale of the East Florida Expedition:

> I was going to seize a vast country in order to give France a port near the outlet of the Gulf of Mexico free of the timid and cowardly courts of a degraded people [i.e., the United States] where daring privateersmen might have been commissioned; a port that might have been turned into a North American entrepôt for the sale of our prizes and where our colonial products might have been exchanged for those of the United States; a port where the live oak and cedar might have built you rot-proof naval fortresses at practically no expense and from whence the infamous brigands from Jamaica and the Bahama Islands might have been chastened.[7]

---

[7] Translated from MANGOURIT, *Mémoir*, pp. 16–17.

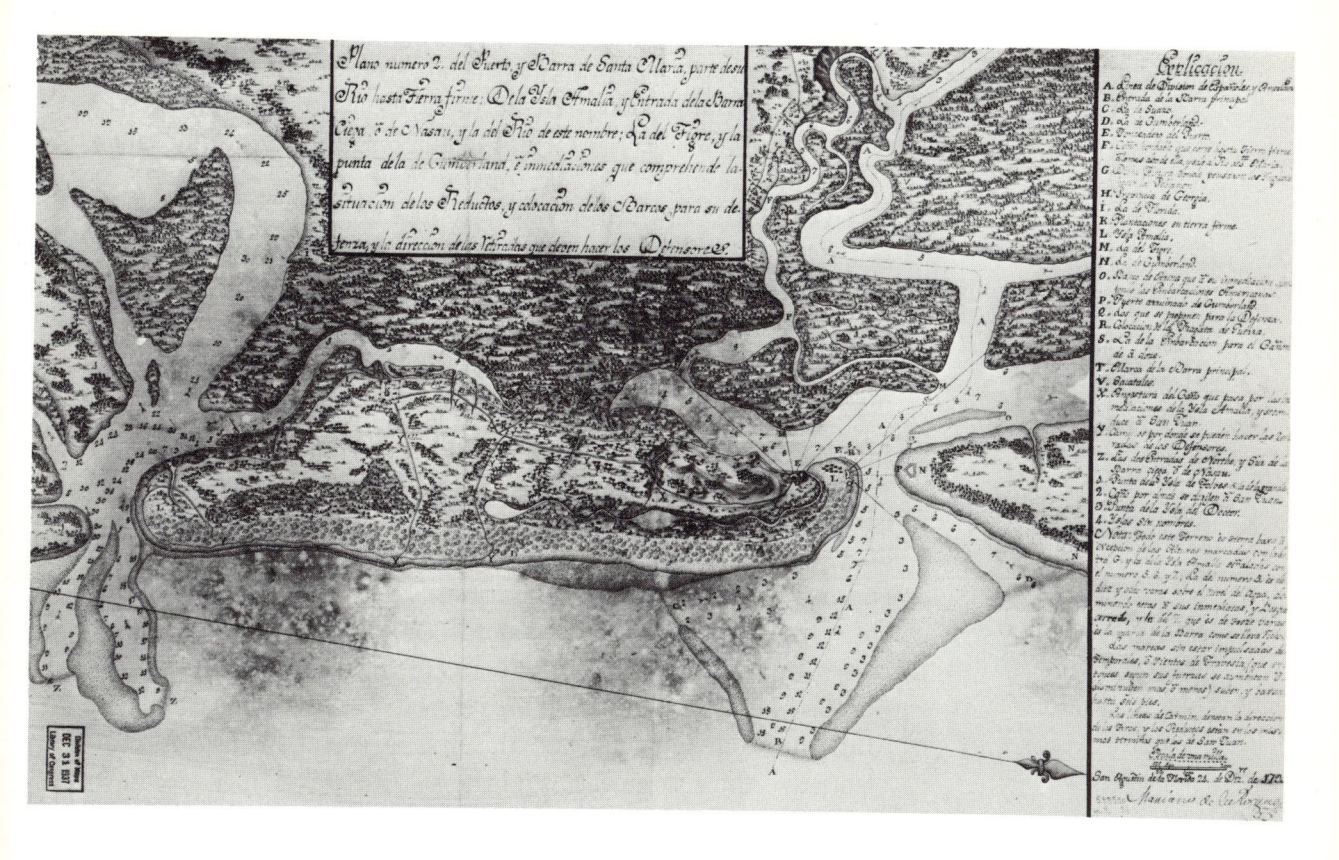

An attack on Amelia Island, however, required a seagoing force not only to carry assault troops but to guard the beaches from interference by Spanish and British naval units. In the past these had been conspicuous by their absence, but this was no guarantee against their sudden appearance. Repeated requests to Genêt for frigates to cover the landing were of no avail.

Thus by the end of 1793 Mangourit had begun frantically to cast about for naval support in the form of French privateers. Few were to be found and these were small in size. From Charleston on November 18, 1793, a Bernardino Sanchez wrote to his brother in Saint Augustine that only three French privateers were then in port. Two of them were careened, while the other was involved in a dispute over the division of prize money. Only one raider based at the port was known to be at sea.[8] On January 4, 1794, the number of French privateers at the port of Charleston was increased by the arrival of the 16-gun

Saint Marys in 1791. "Plano numero 2 del Puerto y Barra de Santa María. . . . San Agustin de la Florida, 24 Diz.re de 1791." From map in the Library of Congress.

---

[8] In a letter from the Governor of Florida to the Captain General of Cuba, Florida and Louisiana, December 10, 1793, *East Florida Papers*, vol. 24.

schooner *le Lascazas*, Branzon, bearing a Saint Domingue commission. Captain Branzon, anxiously seeking the whereabouts of a prize he had taken earlier and sent into Savannah, was relieved to find her, the Jamaican vessel *Friendship*, safely riding at anchor.[9]

To the harassed consul, the arrival of *le Lascazas* was a windfall. Making use of the powers vested in him by Minister Genêt, he promptly requisitioned *le Lascazas* for the Florida expedition, handed out provisional commissions to Branzon and his chief lieutenant, Langlois, and drafted her crew into the French Navy. This action clearly did not set well with men predisposed for privateering, and *le Lascazas* proved to be a most troublesome asset. The end of January saw Branzon and his lieutenant complaining about the burdens imposed upon them by the lack of a sufficient afterguard, while the crew presented a never-ending problem of insubordination.[10] In the meantime the consul sought to add to his naval force by the purchase of other prizes brought by French privateers into Charleston for disposal. The choice of suitable vessels was limited, but finally Mangourit singled out two: the first of these was *le Lascazas'* own prize the *Friendship,* and the second was *Minerva* sent in by the French privateer *l'Atalante*.[11]

On January 14 Mangourit reported to Genêt the situation of his naval force under the heading, "Etat de nos forces en effet ou en espérance à Charleston."[12] The vessels named were very possibly those referred to by Bernardino Sanchez.

---

[9] Branzon had called in at Savannah bar on December 29 and, not finding his prize, had proceeded to Charleston the next day. (*Georgia Gazette*, January 2, 1794; *South-Carolina State-Gazette*, January 4, 1794.)

[10] *The Mangourit Correspondence*, pp. 612–613.

[11] *Minerva* entered Charleston on January 4, 1794. Her history, a curious one, illustrates the vicissitudes of privateering. Originally of French registry, she was built in Saint Domingue as *la Minerve* in 1792. At the outbreak of Franco-British hostilities she was one of the first vessels in that colony to be commissioned as a privateer. When the British landed at Jérémie in 1793, *la Minerve* managed to break out, only to be captured in the Windward Passage. Sent out by her British owners as the privateer *Minerva* under the red ensign, she was recaptured by the French privateer *l'Atalante* and sent for adjudication to Charleston, where she came under Mangourit's eye. *L'Atalante*, shortly after dispatching *Minerva* to Charleston, was in turn captured, having mistaken HM Postal Packet *Antelope* for a merchantman. (See JAMES, *The Naval History of Great Britain*, vol. 2, pp. 110–111.) James and the *South-Carolina State-Gazette* (January 5, 1795), state that *l'Atalante* was one of the original Charleston commissioned vessels, but no substantiation of this has been found.

[12] *The Mangourit Correspondence*, p. 605.

In addition to *le Lascazas,* noted as carrying at this time 18 6-pounders and 120 men, Mangourit included *Friendship,* under her former name *le Robert,* with 16 guns and 50 men;[13] *Minerva,* with 8 guns, 6 swivels, and 40 men; *la Sans Pareille,* whose armament had been reinforced by 2 swivels and 4 broadside guns; *l'Industrie,* with 12 guns, 2 howitzers, and 50 men; and an unnamed vessel, supposed to be enroute from Martinique, with 12 guns and 40 men.

The entire flotilla was expected to be ready for operations by the beginning of February, a time determined by completion of repairs to *l'Industrie,* which had grounded while returning from a cruise.

Mangourit proved overoptimistic, however, about the state of readiness of his naval force. Actually, Carvin's participation in the expedition was far from settled; in fact, at the last moment, the consul found it necessary to requisition *l'Industrie.*[14] A vessel promised by Bouteille never did show up, while *le Robert* (ex-*Friendship*) which had been sent to Saint Domingue for a commission, returned to Charleston under a new name, *la Montagne,* too late to participate in the expedition. As for *Minerva,* as late as March 5 Mangourit was still impatiently awaiting Genêt's permission to purchase her.[15] *Le Lascazas* continued a constant problem because of her bickering crew and ineffective officers.

While Mangourit agonized over Genêt's evasiveness on the supply of promised naval reinforcements, new problems were being posed by the Governor of Georgia, who was having second thoughts on the recruiting of troops in his State for the Florida expedition. It seemed wise, therefore, to allow Bouteille to go cruising off the Florida and Cuban coasts in order to keep his crew occupied with raiding and to develop intelligence on the state of the defenses of Saint Augustine.

In the first week of February *la Sans Pareille* captured the Spanish vessel *la Santa Isabella,* from Havana for Saint Augustine, and sent her into Charleston with a 4-man prize crew. If the value of the vessel as a prize was small, she was an excellent

---

[13] The history of *le Robert* curiously parallels that of *la Minerve.* She too had started life as a French privateer, had been captured by a New Providence privateer, was condemned at Nassau and fitted out as the letter of marque *Friendship,* under which name she was captured by *le Lascazas.* (See *Stannick* v. *the ship Friendship* in (Bee, *Reports,* p. 40.)

[14] *The Mangourit Correspondence,* pp. 650–651.   [15] Ibid., p. 628.

propaganda piece. The docility toward the prize crew shown by the 32 men that she carried from the Third Company of Havana Volunteers augured well for the ease with which the Spanish possessions could be seized.[16] By Mangourit's count *la Santa Isabella* was Bouteille's fifteenth prize, and the captured Spanish seamen related that when last seen, *la Sans Pareille* was hot on the heels of yet another Spanish vessel.

But elation gave way to anxiety over the future of the expedition when reports arrived that a British armed vessel of 14 guns was standing off Tybee Roads and two heavily armed Liverpool Letters of Marque were lying at Savannah.

While Mangourit vainly tried to get *le Lascazas* off to sea to meet the British challenge, the British consular officer at Charleston, Mr. Shoolbred, sent off to learn the character of the British man-of-war. She proved to be HM frigate *Hussar*, Captain Rupert George, on a routine patrol.[17] Arrangements were made for *Hussar* to take under convoy five British merchantmen that had been held in a state of blockade by the French privateers.

Hussar appeared off Charleston on February 7 and for two days patrolled the approaches to the harbor in the hope of intercepting French raiders. On the 10th she signalled for the British vessels to leave the harbor and then stood to the north with the convoy.

Six days later a Spanish snow under a French prize crew stood across the bar. This was the vessel which the Spanish sailors had reported as under chase by Bouteille. In addition to some 130 dispirited Spanish troops the snow carried the considerable sum of 187,000 Spanish dollars as payroll for the Spanish garrison at Saint Augustine.[18] As for Jean Bouteille, shortly after

---

[16] Ibid., pp. 606–607. Mangourit reported that many of the prisoners wanted to join the French forces after they had been duly enlightened on the subject of their slavery to the Spanish "Capet," but that French law prevented their enlistment. Could they not be used on earthworks ashore? Their arms and uniforms were very attractive; could they not be purchased? The problem of incarcerating the Spanish prisoners proved a knotty one that was solved temporarily by turning *le Lascazas* into a prison ship.

[17] HMS *Hussar*, Captain Rupert George, was attached to the Halifax Squadron. She patroled and offered convoy escort in the area from Halifax to Bermuda and New Providence. Details of her movements are from Public Records Office, London, Admiralty 51/452, part 8, HMS *Hussar*, Captain's log.

[18] The prize was met entering Charleston on February 16 by Captain Garman of the *Philadelphia Packet* and was reported in the Philadelphia *General Advertiser*, March 28, 1794 (see also *The Mangourit Correspondence*, p. 612).

his spectacular coup he came ashore for a spell to bask in the admiration of Charleston's "san culottes," to partake of the lively social life of the city, and to expand his privateering interests.

The departure, soon after the safe arrival of the Spanish prize, of the British frigate and the two Liverpool Letters of Marque lifted the threat to the Florida expedition. Local prospects for the success of the expedition were bright, and developments on the diplomatic front were even more promising, for by the beginning of 1794 American anti-British feeling had risen to hysterical proportions. Even as early as September 1793, British depredations on American trade had reached the point that Thomas Jefferson instructed United States Minister to Great Britain Thomas Pinckney to protest in the strongest terms. His instructions echoed a large and growing sector of American opinion: "Great Britain might indeed feel the desire of starving an enemy nation, but she can have no right to do so at our loss, nor of making us the instrument of it." [19]

Great Britain's answer, however, was to draw the noose of maritime restrictions even tighter. The Order-in-Council of November 6, 1793, extended the grounds for seizure of neutral shipping, and the British colonial privateers reacted enthusiastically. Colonial vice-admiralty courts, notably those of New Providence, Saint Kitts, and Saint Vincents, rapidly became notorious for their juridical sleight of hand.

In the wake of British military operations in the French Windward Islands, wholly illegal prize courts were even created to deal with neutral shipping trapped in the harbors of the French Islands. The "Martinique cases," involving American vessels condemned at that island and constituting the largest single group in the later adjustment of British spoliations of 1793, were characterized by United States Commissioner Bayard as "shameful and abominable." [20] The corrupting hand of Britain could be discerned everywhere. Even Britain's role in bringing about a treaty between Portugal and Algiers took on a sinister cast. To some this act portended a diabolical plot

---

[19] MOORE, *International Adjudications*, vol. 4, p. 16.

[20] Ibid., p. 38. Justice Marriott, sitting on the *Relief* case, returned that vessel to her owners with costs and damages and the comment that "the captors were in a great hurry to sell these vessels and pocket the money . . . . as to [General] Sir Charles Grey, he may have little to do with the business, but Sir John Jervis [later Lord St. Vincent] ought, and must have known better" (ibid., pp. 53–54, 57).

Facsimile copy, dated 24 November 1884, in United States National Archives (record group 77, no. 7) of a map of Saint Augustine dated December 24, 1791, in the Archives of the Dirección de Ingenieros, Madrid.

to unleash the fury of the Algerine corsairs against United States trade in the Mediterranean.[21]

When the second session of the Second Congress met at Philadelphia on December 2, 1793, the Federalist Administration noted with alarm a loss of support which some saw as a reflection of anti-British sentiment that was causing growing unrest among the electorate. It was not until December 16 that the growing maritime problem was faced in a rather oblique manner through the reading of the Secretary of State's report concerning the privileges and restrictions on the commerce of the United States. Almost three weeks were spent in an effort to avoid coming to grips with the ominous situation. Finally, on January 3, 1794, Madison's seven resolutions were taken up.[22] The chief tenor of these resolutions was that England was to be subjected to economic pressure until she would come to heel. The ensuing ten-day debate produced a deeper split between the parties but no decision could be made on the resolutions, and definitive action was further delayed.

In the meantime the drift toward war with Great Britain continued. By early February Charlestonians, like the majority of other Americans, were convinced that war was not only inevitable but imminent.[23] By the beginning of March, when Congress again took under consideration Madison's seven resolutions, further procrastination was out of the question. British depredations had practically halted the booming West Indian trade, and at New York unemployment among seamen grew as owners and masters refused to risk their vessels and cargoes against the odds of British capture and confiscation, or of long detentions which could prove equally ruinous.[24] And the situation was further exacerbated by the deterioration of the tense situation along the Canadian frontier and at the Western Posts, and by an outbreak of Algerian seizures of American shipping in the Mediterranean.

On March 4 the Congress cautiously took a first step in answer to British provocations in the form of a bill providing

---

[21] BASSETT, *The Federalist System*, p. 113. For correspondence reflecting this see *Instructions to the British Minister to the United States, 1791–1812*, pp. 49–50.

[22] *American State Papers*, vol. 1, pp. 300–400.

[23] *The Mangourit Correspondence*, p. 612. Appearance of HMS *Hussar* off the Charleston bar resulted in a near panic among American shipping, both ocean and coastal, in the harbor and caused many sailings to be postponed.

[24] MCMASTER, *History*, vol. 2, pp. 167–170, treats at some length the effect of British policy on the maritime centers of the United States.

for the fortification of harbors, and a week later it cleared the way for later creation of the United States Navy by authorizing the building of six frigates. The climax of American reaction to British provocations was finally reached on March 25, when President Washington read to Congress two letters from Fulwar Skipworth, American consular agent at Martinique. The letters detailed the extent of the losses suffered by American merchants in the capture of not only Martinique but the other West Indian islands seized by British forces. A 30-day embargo on all shipping in American harbors was immediately voted pending clarification of events in the Caribbean and before its expiration a 30-day extension was voted.

The action of Congress seemed fully vindicated when on March 28 the news of Britain's revised Order-in-Council of November 6, 1793, became public. The provisions of this decree even outraged the strongly Federalist mercantile community of New England. The Reverend William Bentley, tireless diarist and staunch Federalist, commenting on the actions of Congress, recorded that "a privateer is already up in Becket's yard and several are said to be engaged."[25] On every hand it was agreed that the country was as good as at war with England.

At Charleston, as elsewhere, the democratic societies were in the forefront of preparations for all eventualities. Militia units such as the Charleston Irish Volunteers, the Republican Battery, and the Cadette Battery sprang up, and much time was spent in drilling. As had earlier happened during the fitting out of the Jamaican sloop *Advice,* the clubs set themselves up as watchdogs, this time on behalf of the enforcement of the embargo. On one occasion the Charleston Republican Society, hearing that the British brig *Liberty* had managed to escape from the harbor just prior to publication of the embargo proclamation, fitted out a vessel which successfully recovered the brig.[26] But the excitement of warlike preparations gave way to a noticeable gloom as April passed. As the consequences of hostilities with Great Britain became clearer, Congress became more and more loath to make any decision that might have fatal consequences.

In France, meanwhile, with the establishment of the Jacobin dictatorship under Robespierre in the summer of 1793, supreme

---

[25] *The Diary of William Bentley, D.C.,* vol. 2 (January 1793–December 1802). Hereafter cited as Bentley, *Diary.*

[26] For the details of this incident, see *The City Gazette,* April 10, 1794.

control passed into the hands of a ten-man Committee of Public Safety that undertook ruthlessly to reconstruct the nation from the shambles of civil war—an effort that was accompanied by systematic stamping out of all opposition through the machinery of the Terror.

Eager to exploit the Anglo-American tension, the Committee of Public Safety reviewed Franco-American relations. Minister Genêt, whose conduct had outraged the United States Government and caused it on August 4, 1793, to revoke his exequatur and demand his recall, had failed miserably to carry out the fundamental part of his mission—negotiation of a commercial treaty. Instead, he had allowed himself to be diverted by dreams of military glory which were frustrated by the political intrigue and anarchy that prevailed among the French naval forces in North America. Genêt, moreover, was an appointee of the execrated Brissotins, betrayers of the Revolution, sufficient cause in itself for his liquidation.

To replace Genêt, Jean Antoine Joseph Fauchet was chosen to head a commission armed with the most positive instructions: every means were to be employed to smooth over Franco-American relations, and a most important step toward this goal was to assure and rigorously enforce a rigid respect for United States neutrality. In addition, Fauchet was to concentrate on securing the commercial treaty that Genêt had botched. He was also to obtain supplies of all kind and to arrange for large-scale purchases of grain vitally needed to replenish France's granaries, exhausted by a combination of bad harvest and civil war in La Vendée.

Toward the end of January 1794, Hampton Roads, the port of Norfolk, Virginia, had begun to bustle with activity as arrival of the French sloop-of-war *le Brutus*[27] brought news of Fauchet's approach. *Le Brutus* was followed by a squadron of five French men-of-war under the command of Rear Admiral Jean Van Stabel.[28] On February 8 the frigate *la Charente* arrived at Norfolk to set ashore Citizen Fauchet and his fellow commissioners. Unlike his predecessor, Fauchet did not dally but departed posthaste for Philadelphia, a journey that took

---

[27] Not to be confused with *le Brutus Français*, about which see below, p. 69.
[28] Vessels constituting the squadron were the frigates *le Tigre*, of 80 guns; *le Jean Bart*, 74; *la Concorde* and *la Semillante*, 40; and the brig *le Papillon*. See the Philadelphia *General Advertiser* for January 29 and February 21, 1794.

nearly two weeks, thanks to bad weather and execrable roads. On February 22 he was presented to President Washington and on March 2 he formally relieved *ci-devant* Citizen Genêt of his duties as Minister Plenipotentiary.[29]

Seeking the quickest and most public means of proving to the Government at Philadelphia the sincerity of France's respect for the neutrality of the United States, Fauchet inserted in the *American Daily Advertiser* for March 6 a proclamation which was subsequently widely copied:

> *In the name of the French Republic*
> Every Frenchman is forbid [sic] to violate the neutrality of the United States. All commissions or authorizations intended to infringe that neutrality are revoked and are to be returned to the agents of the French republic.
> Philadelphia, Ventose 16, second year of the French republic one and indivisible (March 6, 1794, O.S.) The Minister plenipotentiary of the French republic,
> [Signed] JN FAUCHET.[30]

Then Citizen Fauchet began to study the dossiers of France's consular officers in the light of his Government's new policy. The file of Citizen Mangourit required urgent consideration.

At Charleston, by early February, Mangourit had heard rumors of Genêt's possible replacement. If these were true, it must have seemed highly probable to Mangourit that his own recall would follow. His correspondence took on a note of increasing urgency and at times hysteria. On March 5, apparently still unaware of Fauchet's arrival, no less of Genêt's replacement, he wrote to the latter, expressing fear that the expedition might be abandoned, and then flatly announced that the invasion date was set for April 10.[31] It seems clear that by making this decision Mangourit hoped to forestall any change in orders that either Genêt or a new Minister at Philadelphia might make and, if luck were with him, to present either one or the other with a *fait accompli* in East Florida. To this announcement Mangourit added a plea for ships, arms, munitions, and provisions, and complained that delays in obtaining these essential needs made it ever more difficult to hold his forces together.

---

[29] Although Fauchet was directed to bundle Genêt back to Paris to answer for his handling of the mission, the very government that Genêt had attacked with such intemperance granted him political asylum.

[30] This notice first appeared in the Charleston papers on March 27 (see p. 38).

[31] *The Mangourit Correspondence*, p. 627.

But the climate at Charleston seemed to be changed: citizens were becoming less tolerant of the high jinks and brawling of the privateersmen. A riot which broke out in a Charleston theatre on March 17 saw no less a personage than Captain Branzon and his trusty Lieutenant Langlois dragged off to jail and fined for their complicity in the fray.[32] The crew of *le Lascazas* had got so out of hand that Mangourit attempted to control the flow of liquor to the French seaman by reminding tavern keepers that they extended credit to the crews of French vessels at their own risk. The French republic did not recognize claims against anticipated prize money.[33] The success of the consul's warning is open to doubt.

By March 23, Mangourit, if his erratic dating can be relied upon, finally heard of Genêt's recall and, very possibly, of his own. To Genêt he expressed his regrets and hoped that the former minister would speak a few kind words to the "incorruptible" Robespierre.[34] But Mangourit's regrets did not affect his determination to press on. He immediately set about rushing preparations to such a point that Fauchet could not possibly order the expedition cancelled.

In his first letter to Fauchet, Mangourit, fearing that the inevitable enemies had already reached the ears of the new minister, sought to reassure him of his zeal for the revolutionary cause.[35] He not only dismissed as incredible the possibility that the new commissioners could intend to call off the Florida expedition, but went on to urge the appointment of a henchman, one Frémin, then acting vice-consul at Savannah, to a post to be created on the United States side of the Saint Marys River, where it would be handy to the new conquests.

---

[32] *South-Carolina Gazette*, March 19, 1794; *The City Gazette*, March 20, 1794.

[33] *The City Gazette*, March 21, 1794. Mangourit cited chapter and verse of French law which disclaimed responsibility of the French Republic for debts incurred in advance of prize money.

[34] *The Mangourit Correspondence*, p. 638.

[35] As was the case in all American cities where French refugees gathered in numbers, intrigue between the varying shades of political opinion was rampant. Strife within the Charleston Patriotic Society was recorded by the *State Gazette of South-Carolina* as early as December 3, 1793. Mangourit had been branded as "an intriguant and a promoter of discord." Enemies held his newspaper articles to be inflammatory in the extreme. Denunciations made to Fauchet to this effect certainly affected the decision on the Consul's replacement. In his *Mémoir*, Mangourit refers bitterly to the maneuverings of partisan groups, many of them doubtlessly infiltrated by British *agents provocateurs*.

To Fauchet's demands of late March that *le Lascazas* be sent north to Hampton Roads, where she was urgently needed to strengthen the escort for the grain convoy,[36] Mangourit answered that he regretted being unable to comply: not only was the corvette allocated to his own particular service, she was then at sea on a training cruise.[37] In fact, however, *le Lascazas* was still in port embroiled in her interminable crew problems and Mangourit's orders to Branzon to get to sea were not dated until March 27.

On the very day that *le Lascazas* was scheduled to sail, the thunder and lightning of Fauchet's public circular letter of March 6 struck in the local press.[38] Mangourit dodged agilely. An urgent meeting of the leaders of the Florida expedition was assembled in a council of war on March 29 to ponder the nature of Fauchet's injunction.[39] Was this surprising document in truth an English ruse? Perhaps it had been concocted by Fauchet in conjunction with the United States Government to mislead the English and Spanish as the first step in America's declaration of war. Some were suspicious about the dating of the document and made a point of the fact that it was not in accord with the new revolutionary calendar. If the purpose of the declaration was really to stop the invasion, why had not the new minister sent an express to that purpose when he first stepped ashore? In any case, the feeling was general that the injunction against recruiting quite eliminated the Florida expedition from the intent of the declaration. After all, was not all its recuiting carried on outside the boundaries of the United States? The clinching argument against the applicability of the declaration, however, was that the invasion date had been set prior to the issuance of the printed circular.

The council of war finally decided that it could not find the slightest excuse to stop the execution of the enterprise and agreed to press on with the greatest diligence and secrecy. Only Colonel Bert dissented and expressed grave doubts about

---

[36] *Correspondence of the French Ministers to the United States, 1791–1797*, Commissioners to Ministers of Foreign Affairs, May 20, 1794, p. 346.

[37] *The Mangourit Correspondence*, p. 645.

[38] See *The City Gazette*, March 27, 1794.

[39] *The Mangourit Correspondence*, pp. 629–632. Branzon's name appears among those who were present at the council of war. The details that follow are derived from the minutes of the council.

the success of the enterprise without the essential ingredient of seapower to cover the landings and prevent intervention by enemy sea forces.

The letter which Mangourit wrote to Fauchet on March 29 explained the proceedings of the council of war and predicted the fate awaiting French privateering operations out of American ports in spite of the Franco-American *rapprochement* inaugurated by Fauchet. Ending with a persuasive argument, Mangourit urged:

> The ports of Florida will be of the greatest utility to France in wartime. The privateering commissions which we will be able to issue there will not be subject to the interference of the United States. The armed vessels which will sail from Florida will enjoy all the advantages that they should have had in those [i.e., United States] ports. The St. Mary's [river], being capable of receiving entire fleets, will especially facilitate our maritime operations.[40]

Only five days before Mangourit's letter of March 29, the *State Gazette of South-Carolina* reported the receipt of a Treasury Department Circular Letter which directed collectors of the custom to take inventories of all vessels and cargoes which had been captured by illegal privateers and brought into American ports, and to consult with the consuls of nations whose vessels had been seized, with the view of appointing appraisers to arrive at a valuation of damages suffered.[41] The Secretary of War had even ordered that the Spanish brig *San José*[42] be delivered up to her owners because her capture was considered collusive.

Ignoring Fauchet's orders to cease and desist from any further attempts to execute any design that might infringe on United States neutrality, Mangourit wrote the Minister on March 30 that everything was ready—supplies, ammunition, and treaties with the Indians. Two transports were ready to leave on April 4 and the landing would be made on April 10 Then, incomprehensibly, he wrote, "Nous attendons la flotille et la Floride est à nous . . . Ah! Citoyen, ce projet si vous envoyez une flotille. . . ."[43]

---

[40] Ibid. Translation of report of Assembly of Leaders of the Expedition at Charleston, March 29, 1794.

[41] *South-Carolina State-Gazette*, March 24, 1794.

[42] Undoubtedly this is the prize made by Bouteille called *San Joseph* which featured in the important admiralty case of *Castello* v. *Bouteille, et al.*, and treated at length below. The case was being argued in court at the very time.

[43] *The Mangourit Correspondence*, p. 645.

The following day another letter to Fauchet was dashed off containing more sermonizing, urging, logic, and wheedling on the subject of the invasion. Forgetting that he had told his superior that *le Lascazas* was at sea he announced her departure with the transports. Again he hammered at his need for a fleet. Genêt had promised him one on February 2. Where was it? Send it. More money was needed; the war scare had driven the price of supplies out of sight.

But even if the promised flotilla had existed, it is certain that Mangourit had no intention of waiting for it. On March 27 the consul issued orders to Branzon on the subject of the Saint Marys landings: *le Lascazas* was to cruise off the coast, "not too far off the bar;" on April 4, he was to close the harbor, send in a boat and be prepared to escort the transports southward. If Branzon should arrive off Saint Marys before April 9, he was to cruise off the mouth of the river and keep it bottled up. Detailed instructions were given on how contact was to be made with the "revolutionary legion." Knowing his man and *le Lascazas'* crew, Mangourit could not refrain from the injunction, "Don't stray off chasing prizes." [44]

Mangourit's vexation with Branzon and the corvette *le Lascazas* was compounded by further troubles with his other armed ships. As late as March 30 he could count on only the two transports he had mentioned earlier to Fauchet. He had been unsuccessful in his attempt to purchase the prize *Minerva*. This vessel was finally bought in by Jean Bouteille, who placed Captain Hervieux in command and sent her off cruising under some sort of commission. Both Bouteille and Carvin continued to cruise during the Fauchet - Mangourit duel, although from the nature of their prizes it may be presumed that to some extent they were cooperating with Mangourit.[45]

With only four days remaining before Captain Branzon was scheduled to appear off Charleston bar to collect the invasion fleet, Mangourit was still frantically trying to assemble shipping. In a letter to Carvin dated March 31 the consul congratulated the privateer captain on his successful cruise and refreshed Car-

---

[44] Ibid., pp. 643–644.

[45] On March 16 *la Sans Pareille* returned to port accompanied by the Spanish prize *San José*, mentioned above (*South-Carolina State-Gazette*, March 18, 1794). Shortly before March 29 Carvin brought his *l'Industrie* back to Charleston after a successful cruise which netted the Spanish sloop *Emmanuel* (*South-Carolina State-Gazette*, March 28, 1794).

vin's memory about former discussions concerning his participation in the East Florida Expedition. That campaign, announced Mangourit, was about to be realized and Florida was about to be snatched from Spanish tyranny. At first he elaborately protested his conviction of Carvin's patriotism. Then he insinuated that a loan would be in order (Carvin had taken a particularly valuable prize). Finally, after dismissing any thought that Carvin would refuse to cooperate, he peremptorily requisitioned *l'Industrie*, "en vertu de l'article 23 de la Loi du 11 8bre, 1793," and ordered him to join forces with *le Lascazas*.[46]

In addition to listing Bouteille's *la Sans Pareille* and recently purchased *la Minerve* (ex-*Minerva*) and Carvin's *l'Industrie* as ready for sailing, Mangourit mentioned a fourth vessel, the schooner *l'Ami de la Pointe-à-Pitre*,[47] under the command of William Talbot.

Whether all, or indeed any, of the vessels other than *le Lascazas* sailed on schedule cannot be verified. It is known, however, that *la Sans Pareille* was still in port on the eve of the rendezvous off Charleston bar, for her crew was involved in yet another of those fracases that with increasing frequency were trying the patience of Charlestonians.[48] But it seems likely that none of the privateers listed were in port by April 7, for on that day, from the same express which brought news of the Presidential embargo of March 26, Citizen Fonspertuis stepped ashore, sent by Fauchet to relieve Mangourit as consul general at Charleston for the French Republic.[49]

---

[46] *The Mangourit Correspondence*, pp. 650–651.

[47] Ex-*Fair Play* (see p. 56). The appearance of this vessel, to become one of Charleston's regulars, was heralded by the arrival of a Spanish prize consigned to her on March 16. The *South-Carolina State-Gazette*, March 18, 1794, referred to her as the *Santa Jacta* (possibly a misreading of a manuscript abbreviation "Santa Jac^{ta}[Jacinta]" and to her captor as *Des Amis*. Talbot made his entry into Charleston between March 20 and 30 and during that period was included in the expedition. Whether Mangourit managed to pry out of Talbot the 15,000 dollars cash reported to be on board the prize is not known.

[48] See, *South-Carolina State-Gazette*, April 4, 1794.

[49] While part of Fauchet's instructions related to the replacement of those consuls and agents who were particularly involved in transgressions of United States neutrality, he was actually unequipped to send a man of sufficient calibre to substitute for Mangourit. Fonspertuis, who had accompanied Fauchet as a minor chancellery official, remains a relative unknown whose chief qualification seems to have been his removal from the Canary Islands as consul at the request of the Spanish Government. According to the custom of the era he was known simply by his last name.

While there can be no doubt that at first Fonspertuis entered with exemplary zeal into the task of enforcing his superior's orders, Mangourit's delays in turning over the consulate's records and Fonspertuis' inability, because of the embargo proclamation, to charter a vessel to pursue the Florida squadron prevented him from immediately effecting the most important part of his mission—the recall of the Florida expedition.[50]

Not until April 14 did the new consul manage to charter the schooner *Hawke* and to arrange with the deputy collector of the port for a coastwise clearance for Saint Marys in Georgia.[51] Ex-consul Mangourit, whose departure gave rise to eloquent expressions of regret from some of the leading Charlestonians,[52] was hustled on board *Hawke*, and her supercargo Alexandre Bolchos—soon to build a reputation of his own as a successful privateer commander—was ordered to seek out *le Lascazas* and bring about abandonment of the expedition. Thereafter Mangourit and his suite were to be transferred to the corvette, which in turn was to proceed forthwith to Philadelphia so that the ex-consul could report in person to Minister Fauchet on his activities. This was duly accomplished.

The invasion as planned proved a fiasco. When *le Lascazas* was finally located, Branzon had been standing on and off the mouth of the Saint Marys for 17 days, unable to make contact with the Florida Legion, even though it was reported that the Legion was in the immediate vicinity and was expected momentarily. Actually, a small group of American and Floridian filibusterers managed to establish themselves on the southern bank of the Saint Marys River, never losing hope that a French reinforcement would come to their relief.[53]

What roles the privateers *la Sans Pareille, la Minerve, l'Industrie,* and *l'Ami de la Pointe-à-Pitre* played in the aborted

---

[50] He did, however, according to his instructions, release English prisoners that Mangourit had been illegally detaining in a prison hulk in Charleston harbor, and reparations were duly made. See *The City Gazette*, May 15, 1794, which printed an extract of Fonspertuis-Fauchet correspondence; also mentioned was the fact that *le Lascazas* was not in Charleston when Fonspertuis arrived.

[51] Under the terms of the embargo, coastwise vessels as well as foreign public vessels and privateers were allowed to clear customs.

[52] In his *Mémoir*, Mangourit printed at length testimonials to the excellence of his stewardship of France's interests during his term in office. The signatures subscribing to the testimonials constitute a virtual "Who's Who" of Charleston's most dedicated Republicans.

[53] See *Correspondence of the French Ministers to the United States*, 1791–1797, p. 827, Adet to Minister of Foreign Affairs, February 9, 1796.

invasion is not certain. No mention of them was made in the account of the locating of *le Lascazas*. It is possible that they had been dispatched on scouting missions when no contact was made with the Legion, or even more likely—from the succession of prizes that entered Charleston by the end of April—they had gone off on raiding expeditions of their own.

On April 27 *la Sans Pareille* arrived at Charleston, her captain lamenting that because of a shortage of crew he had been forced to pass up two Spanish vessels. She was followed the next day by two of her prizes, the British snow *Susannah* and the schooner *Ann*.[54] On May 2 an unnamed Spanish brig of 10 guns and 35 men, laden with cargo, entered as prize to *la Sans Pareille* and finally, on May 6, arrived still another Spanish vessel, *Del Pelao* (*Del Sillaro?*), consigned to the same privateer. All were passed through the French consular court and condemned.[55]

Both Carvin and Talbot subsequently returned with interesting prizes of their own, to be noted below. As for the schooner *Hawke*, once her duty was completed she blithely ignored her coastwise clearance and made directly for Port-de-Paix in Saint Domingue. There on June 10 she was sold to Alexandre Bolchos, who had gone out in her as supercargo, and was commissioned on the same day as the French privateer *la Parisienne*.[56]

On June 27 *la Parisienne* entered Charleston in company with her British prize *Prosperity*, and almost immediately became involved in the District Court of South Carolina over the legality of her prize and the legitimacy of her commission. *La Parisienne* survived the suit to become one of the longest lived of the Charleston privateers and one of the most successful as well.

Fonspertuis' attempt to call off the Florida expedition coincided with the sailing of the great French convoy on April 17, 1794, an event which strained Anglo-American relations to the breaking point. If British minister Hammond skirted making

---

[54] *Susannah* and *Ann* grossed £7,277/5/6, while the Spanish brig, which was estimated at 20,000 Spanish dollars, grossed £4,300/19/8. See *The City Gazette*, May 15, 1794; and *BCC*, Annex J, pp. 612–613.

[55] See *South-Carolina State-Gazette*, April 30, May 2, and May 6, 1794.

[56] Details of the saga of the *Hawke* are gleaned from cases in Bee, *Reports: The United States* v. *Schooner Hawke* (pp. 34–38); *Kelly, Jun.* v. *Schooner Prosperity and Cargo and John Coole* (pp. 38–39); and *British Consul* v. *Schooner Favourite and Alexander Bolchos* (pp. 39–41).

Michel Ange Bernard Mangourit (1752–1829), freemason, revolutionary, pamphleteer, editor, scholar and archeologist, diplomatist, and vice-consul of the French Republic at Charleston, South Carolina, 1792–1794. From a print in the Bureau des Estampes, Bibliothèque Nationale, Paris.

a direct charge of American complicity in allowing the convoy to sail while a general embargo was in effect he nevertheless accused the United States Government of neglect to employ "coercive means" of preventing its departure.[57]

On May 2 and again on May 12 the Reverend Bentley noted the progression toward war in Salem: "A Derby vessel was being set up . . . upon the model of a privateer. . . . Yesterday was launched at Beckett's a schooner built in the form of a privateer . . . another of the same construction to be set up immediately."[58]

None of the privateers being built along the Atlantic coast in March, April, and May 1794 went cruising against the British under American colors, but many did under the tricolor, for, as we shall see, a thriving market came into being for such spe-

---

[57] Attorney General Edmund Randolph, who succeeded Jefferson as Secretary of State in January 1797, had to extricate his Government as best he could. He denied that permission had been granted for the clearance of the convoy and then weakly offered as an extenuating circumstance the distance of Norfolk from the seat of Government, along with the plaintive observation that no formal complaint had ever been received from the British at Philadelphia. (BCC, p. 577).

[58] *The Diary of William Bentley*, vol. 2, pp. 85, 86.

cialized vessels and Charleston became a center for their export to the West Indies.

Even while the French convoy was clearing American waters, President Washington, bent on heading off the war which threatened so ominously, decided to dispatch an envoy extraordinary to London. After some delay, John Jay was chosen for the mission on April 19. The reaction to Jay's mission was mixed at the start. The Philadelphia *General Advertiser* voiced militantly anti-British sentiment in an article which began, "Negotiations, negotiations, is yet the cry of the minority in Congress. . . ." [59] Yet, even though the embargo proved irksome to some, the *American Daily Advertiser,* having earlier decried peace overtures, found it necessary to reprove a demonstration of unemployed seamen marching in the streets of Philadelphia with the advice that they "could get 5–6 shillings as laborers or stonecutters." And in spite of the anti-British furor that arose in May over a lurid episode of British arrogance at Newport, Rhode Island, war fever dwindled rapidly [60] as the appeals by Federalist journals for a sense of proportion on the subject of British villainies made steady headway.

To many contemporary observers the embargo appeared to have done what had been intended, at least as far as the British West Indies were concerned. Island assemblies soon clamored for relief from the acute scarcity of plantation staples and from the glut of tropical produce overflowing their warehouses, a situation certainly the result of the embargo. Governor after Governor yielded, suspending the Navigation Acts for periods of six months to a year and inviting neutral traders to their harbors.

The prize so eagerly sought by the Americans trading to the West Indies, and so maddeningly denied since the treaty of peace with England in 1783 now seemed within reach. It would have been a shame to allow such ripe plums to fall to the neutral Danes and Swedes. To many of the mercantile community in the United States, burdened with depreciated French assignats, with protested bills of exchange, and with vessels immobilized in continental French ports by embargoes, the loss of trade with such fragments of the French West Indian Islands that

---

[59] April 17, 1794.

[60] The British Frigate *Nautilus* was boarded by representatives of the Rhode Island legislature in May when, after several demands had been made, her captain had refused to release several impressed seamen. The Americans were forcibly removed while the British commander promised dire consequences for the trespass upon one of his Britannic Majesty's vessels.

remained would be small compared to the gain from a liberalized trade with the British West Indian Islands.

John Jay, who had sailed for England on May 12 to adjust outstanding differences and to negotiate trade agreements with Great Britain, apparently had succeeded in placing the limited opening of West Indian trade on a permanent basis.

The embargo was allowed to expire without further renewal.[61] Once again the country was divided. Some were glad, others were resentful. The democratic societies, divining the effect on the French cause, shrilled against the renewal of intercourse with Great Britain. The sectional issue was raised by Philadelphia's pro-French *General Advertiser*. "Great News! The Embargo is off—but stop! Great news from whom? For those who have petitioned for an exemption for their *fish*."[62]

But the sound of protest [63] was lost in the bustle of sails being bent and running rigging being overhauled in every port along the Atlantic Coast. At Philadelphia, on the day the embargo ended, 55 vessels dropped down the Delaware, 45 of them cleared for the West Indies alone.[64] About 30 vessels sailed from New York and as many from Baltimore. Within a week after the embargo was lifted, a probable total of 300 vessels cleared out of United States ports.

In Boston the Reverend Bentley philosophized on the irrationality of mercantile man as he observed the busy waterfront:

> May 24:—last day of the Embargo and all busy to prepare to crowd the market: Some enquiring why it was put on? Others why taken off? . . . (S)ome wounded by their losses others exulting in their gains. Among them all not the least sign of public virtue.
>
> May 27:—Vessles against wind and weather striving to get out of the harbor bound to supply the islands from which we have received the greatest Insults. Even a privateer raised on the stocks in resentment was the first to sail with supplies at the risk of the same owners. Never did interest discover its influence more favorably.[65]

---

[61] An attempt was made in Congress to extend the embargo to June 20 on the grounds it was only beginning to have its desired effect.

[62] May 30, 1794.

[63] At Philadelphia and Baltimore, mates and masters of vessels resolved not to go to sea for ten days after the embargo ended as a symbol of their protest to the raising of the embargo (see McMaster, vol. 2, pp. 174-175).

[64] Only three vessels cleared for Europe; the remainder were coasters. Of the 45, all but four were bound for British Islands, and of the four, three were for Saint Croix (neutral); the fourth was for Dutch Saint Eustatius (*General Advertiser*, Philadelphia, May 28, 1794).

[65] *Dairy of William Bentley*, vol. 2, p. 91.

Chapter 3

THE WAY IS CLEARED BY THE UNITED STATES DISTRICT COURT

NORTH OF THE VIRGINIA CAPES FRENCH PRIVATEERING diminished rapidly after mid-April 1794. Many of the privateers that had not accompanied the sailing of Admiral Cambis' squadron from New York in November 1793—on Genêt's ill-fated campaign against the Newfoundland Banks—were drawn off as convoy escorts for the strategically important grain fleet which cleared out of Hampton Roads, April 17, 1794.[1] Still others fell victim to Minister Fauchet's campaign to eliminate infringements on United States neutrality.[2] By the end of the embargo period the newspapers which had once given the French privateers much space contained few allusions to them.[3]

But, as French privateering decreased north of the Virginia Capes, the reverse was happening at Charleston. From the

---

[1] Among the privateers that sailed with the convoy were *la Cornelia* (ex-*la Petite Démocrate*, ex-*Little Sarah*), and *la Carmagnole*, both of which were commissioned into the French Navy, and Captain Molinari's *le Sans Culotte de Marseille*, which had been laid up at Philadelphia during the winter months.

[2] Fauchet was responsible for the detention and later dismantling of the privateer *Van Stabel*, which had been fitted out at Norfolk in March 1794. See Miscellaneous Letters, 1796–1906, U.S. Department of State, Secretary of State to the President, June 30, 1794.

[3] An attack on two British vessels by the French privateer *Liberty* on May 27 seems to constitute the sum total of French activity. These were the ship *Charles* and the schooner *Delight*, reported as captured in the waters of Chesapeake Bay within a mile of the shore. (BCC, Hammond to Randolph, June 5, 1794, pp. 520–522.) Depositions of the masters of the vessels are included.

departure northward of the original "consular privateers" in May 1793, privateering enterprise there had been seemingly the exclusive domain of Jean Bouteille and Jean Baptiste Carvin. By the end of March 1794, new raiders began to make their appearance, some of them converted from the prizes taken by *la Sans Pareille* and *l'Industrie,* and some from prizes sent in by raiders that never appeared at Charleston. In June the number of French privateers increased notably, and Charleston rapidly became the primary base of operations on United States soil for French raiders. To the general reason already adduced to account for this rise of Charleston as a French privateer haven, i.e., proximity to the main sea route between the Caribbean and Europe and the predisposition of Charlestonians for the French cause, might be added the abandonment of the Florida expedition and France's renunciation of any further adventures in that direction.[4] By June 1794, moreover, two particular elements directly concerned in the acceleration of privateering activity had come strongly to the fore. The first of these was a legal decision handed down by the Federal District Court of South Carolina, and the second was the sudden and dramatic reversal of French military fortunes in the West Indies.

The case of *Castello* v. *Bouteille,* heard during the March term of the District Court at Charleston, paved the way for the later influx of French raiders, and it was ironic that the judge who handed down the decision was Thomas Bee. It is difficult to conceive of a man with deeper distaste for the French revolutionary principles being trumpeted through Charleston, or for the brash vulgarity of the defendant in the case, or for the brawling privateersmen who made it dangerous to walk the streets of his native city.[5] Yet, as we will see, Bee's decisions in case after case challenged the findings of the Supreme Court on points essential to the continued prosecution of privateering by the French operating out of Charleston. The details of

---

[4] When in July 1795 Pierre Adet, who replaced Fauchet as French Minister to the United States, attempted to revive French ambitions in Florida, the privateersmen turned notably cool to the project. See below, p. 102.

[5] FISCHER, *The Revolution of American Conservatism*, p. 397. Fischer lists Bee as one of the "Federalists of the Old School." Bee, the scion of a family of lawyers, was educated at Oxford and read law at Lincoln's Inn. He was a man of wealth, and a holder of slaves on a large scale. In the tradition of old Federalists, Thomas Bee devoted a large part of his life to public service. He had received his appointment as U.S. District Judge in 1790.

3: THE WAY IS CLEARED

Castello v. *Bouteille,* as well as the decision, are of interest for the instructive insight they afford into at least one corner of the arsenal of deception and chicanery developed by the French privateersmen and their agents in order to maintain their foothold in Charleston.

The case arose over the seemingly trivial question of the legal status of 50 bales of cotton, against which Captain Castello, formerly master of the Spanish vessel *San José* filed a libel in behalf of the vessel's owners. The *San José* was en route for Cadiz when she was overhauled and captured by the French privateer sloop *Fair Margaret,* Captain Henri Hervieux, on September 22, 1793.[6]

Hervieux made for Cape Fear River with his prize in company, but when he had arrived off Wilmington, North Carolina, news came that the Government at Philadelphia had ordered

Sloop Mediator, *ca. 1745. Model, in the Smithsonian's National Museum of History and Technology, was constructed from the original plans in the National Maritime Museum, Greenwich, England. That the sloop rig was a favorite in the coastwise and West Indian trade to the end of the 18th century seems confirmed by the number of them captured by the French privateers in the period 1793–1802.*

---

[6] *Fair Margaret* is not listed as one of the privateers that frequented the port of Charleston. It is possible that she was one of the first commissioned by Genêt upon his arrival at Charleston. No other prize made by this privateer is known.

or, more properly speaking, requested, that the Government of North Carolina seize *Fair Margaret* as one of those privateers proscribed under the directive of June 5, 1793. Hervieux lost no time in clearing out of Wilmington. Once at sea he headed south with his prize still in company. Off Charleston bar, Hervieux, who had no intention of endangering his prize as at Wilmington, left *San José* to jog on and off shore under her prize crew while he entered port to survey the situation.

Possibly Mangourit put Hervieux in touch with Jean Bouteille, who was in port at the time after his cruise in company with Carvin's *l'Industrie,* but in any event, the two met, and the result of the meeting was not only the solution of Hervieux's dilemma but also the beginning of a fruitful relationship between the two privateersmen, for Bouteille took *la Sans Pareille* to sea, where contact was made with the waiting *San José,* and in due course that vessel was "seized." The two vessels then proceeded in company down the coast of Georgia where the master and crew of *San José* were set ashore to make their way as best they could to Saint Augustine. The vessels then made for Charleston, where the prize was duly entered as belonging to *la Sans Pareille*. She was processed through the consular court, condemned, and cargo and vessel were offered at public sale.

By the time that Captain Castello had doubled back to Charleston, all that remained to proceed against was the 50 bales of cotton, and these he accordingly libeled. Acting in behalf of his owners and freighters, Castello sought restitution of cargo and vessel as well as damages for detention. Bouteille's answer to the libel was a plea to jurisdiction, that is, he questioned the right of the court to act upon the case. He steadfastly maintained the regularity of his commission and, in addition, invoked article 17 of the Treaty of Amity and Commerce of 1778, between France and the United States.

The libelant built his case primarily on the force of the Presidential directives relating to "proscribed" privateers and maintained that *San José,* now *le Saint Joseph,* was in point of fact captured by the *Fair Margaret* and not by *la Sans Pareille*. Judge Bee, however, refused to recognize the authority of the President in this context. According to Bee, who cited the Constitution on the separation of powers, the President's wishes did not have the force of law and hence were not binding. If *Fair Margaret* was indeed the original captor and a proscribed vessel, the libelant must have recourse to the Executive for relief. Thus, by virtue of the decisions in the *William* case in Pennsylvania, and the *Catherine* case in New York,[7] both of which denied admiralty jurisdiction to the Federal Courts, Bee upheld Bouteille's plea to jurisdiction, and Castello's libel was accordingly dismissed.[8]

Bouteille's victory and the circumstances surrounding the entire case must have been gratifying in the extreme to the privateer fraternity. Not a finger had been raised at either the customhouse or the Governor's mansion to seize the proscribed *Fair Margaret* or to prevent the transparent sleight of hand of shifting the Spanish vessel from Hervieux to Bouteille. Bee even refused to look beyond the law to take into account the obvious fraud. All this augured as well for the future of French privateering, as did Bee's denial of Federal jurisdiction over the activities of the French privateers. But Judge Bee's observations on the nature of the Franco-American treaties then being so severely manhandled in the northern courts, held even greater significance. They seemed to be a total reaffirmation of the case that France had been urging from the very beginning of the war. The libelants had sought, by citing the U.S. treaty with the Netherlands, even though *San José*'s registry was Spanish, to establish that the United States owed certain obligations to those nations with whom she was at peace. Judge Bee, however, was of the opinion that the treaty which bound the United States to France was of a more sweeping nature than the others and was designed to be operative "under all circumstances of war and peace with other nations."[9] The treaty with the Netherlands, he held, was specific. It provided for the restitution of vessels recaptured by either party from a common enemy.

It is difficult to establish or fully to assess the influence that this case had in the rash of conspiracy and bald collusion between the French privateersmen and American officials that marked the year 1794, except to note the coincidence. The machinations, chicanery, and thimblerigging indulged in by the

---

[7] For a discussion of these two cases, see JACKSON, "Consular Privateers," pp. 86, 88, 92n.

[8] It may well be argued that the dismissal of Castello's libel was, in fact, based more on the nonlegal force of the Presidential directive than on lack of admiralty jurisdiction. It should be noted also that while this case was being tried, the Supreme Court was hearing the case of *Glass and Appellants* v. *the sloop Betsey*, which resolved the question of admiralty jurisdiction. See above, p. 19.

[9] BEE, *Reports*, pp. 32–33, *Castello* v. *Bouteille, et. al.*

privateer operators, agents, and captains is attested to by the barebone records and correspondence which have survived from the court proceedings of the day. Thus, his Britannic Majesty's acting vice-consul for Georgia, South Carolina, and North Carolina,[10] seeking to protect the interests of his Government and the property of British shipowners and freighters, was not entirely unjustified when he complained of the difficulties of obtaining cooperation from the persons in authority.[11]

Castello v. *Bouteille* prepared the way for the entry of privateersmen whose operations steered the shadow line between legality and outright piracy, veering from one side to the other as circumstances demanded. The relatively simple deception practiced by Jean Bouteille and Henri Hervieux was elaborated with great ingenuity in subsequent days.

While the majority of the Charleston-based privateers at one time or another played fast and loose with the domestic laws of the United States and with the international conventions governing the institution of privateering, few were more consistent and flagrant in this respect than the privateering syndicate involving three Americans—William Talbot, Edward Ballard, and John Sinclair. The saga of this trio, constitutes a perfect vade mecum of the mechanics of rascality as practiced at Charleston between 1794 and 1795. When Colonel Jacob Read, attorney for the libelants of one of the prizes made by Edward Ballard, in open court called that worthy, his officers, and crew a "Band of Lawless pirates," he was not far from the truth.[12]

We have already met William Talbot, whose arrival at Charleston in late March (see p. 41) caused something of a

---

[10] Vice-Consul Benjamin Moodie arrived at Charleston on February 9, 1794, on board the ship *Caroline*, 70 days from London (*South-Carolina State-Gazette*, February 10, 1794). From his correspondence with Lord Grenville (Public Records Office 133, FO 5, 6, f. 127) we learn that his appointment was a temporary one to replace the deputy consul Shoolbred while on leave. The consulship, however, was actually held by Charles Miller, on leave in England for reasons of health. Moodie was subsequently made permanent consul, in which office he served until his death in 1837.

[11] "I . . . will readily lodge remonstrance in such cases [i.e., illegal captures] and with such executives as you may direct; but it does not seem to me that they consider themselves called upon unless a legal process is instituted, and the authority of the Federal court is disputed, which has latterly determined me to apply there, in the first instance, by libel; otherwise, even the court will not consider the complaint cognizable." BCC, p. 593.

[12] See, PHILLIPS, "South Carolina Federalists II," p. 734. This charge so outraged the hot patriots of the democratic club which Ballard frequented, that a threatened duel was narrowly averted.

3 : THE WAY IS CLEARED

stir in privateering circles. His first involvement in privateering is a story often paralleled in those days when Yankee seamen lived in fear of impressment by the Royal Navy and shipmasters faced ruin at the hands of British colonial privateers and prize courts.[13] Talbot was a native of Virginia and a merchant seaman by trade. According to his own account he had espoused the French cause and had taken to privateering under the French flag out of resentment for injuries suffered at the hands of the British: During the early days of the war he had been taken into New Providence, which was notorious for the voraciousness of its privateersmen and the corruption of its prize courts, where he lost his brig and cargo. There and then he "resolved to be indemnified and revenged." [14] Returning to Virginia, he cast about for a berth and, in October 1793, met John Sinclair, who, in partnership with Solomon Nelson of Smithfield and Samuel Reddick, owned the schooner *Fair Play*. They saw in Talbot qualities needed to forward their plans, and Talbot, for his part, found what he was looking for and readily enlisted in the design to convert the schooner to a French privateer. He was to go in her as master and also to receive a share in the vessel.

The prospect of arming and equipping an American vessel as a French privateer at that time was not too promising. The furor over Genêt was at its height. The Act of June 5, 1793, proscribing the American-commissioned French privateers and the increased vigilance of both State and Federal officers all complicated the business. But Samuel Reddick was an American expatriate, a French citizen, and a legal resident of Guadeloupe. The partners agreed that the vessel *Fair Play* would go to Guadeloupe and there take out French registry. Great care was to be exercised to comply in detail with the Ship Registry Act of 1790, so that her subsequent operations would not be jeopardized by some overlooked technicality. In addition, at Guadeloupe Captain Talbot was to become a French citizen to avoid a recurrence of Henfield's fate.

The arming of *Fair Play* for clearance under United States registry constituted no problem, since it was still within the right of any American merchant vessel to sail armed. With her

---

[13] In many ways Talbot's story is similar to that of the implacable anglophobe and privateersman extraordinary, Joshua Barney.

[14] Talbot's experiences, either provided by himself or the result of an interview, appeared in the *American Daily Advertiser*, of Philadelphia, May 16, 1794.

Pilot boat Coureuse *built at New York about 1785. The pilot-boat hull form, with its reputation for speed and weatherliness, was highly regarded for privateering. Relatively inexpensive to build and man, this type of vessel provided a minimum-investment entry into a field that offered quick returns. This one, captured by the British in 1793 was used as a dispatch boat. Sail plan from H. I. Chapelle, "Search for Speed Under Sail" (New York: W. W. Norton, 1968).*

armament, ammunition, and provisions on board, Talbot received his instructions and a power of attorney to sell the vessel. *Fair Play*, with Citizen Reddick as a passenger, must have sailed shortly after October 24. Once at Guadeloupe, Talbot moved with dispatch. On December 28, 1793, he shed his U.S. citizenship and became a citizen of the French Republic. On December 31 Citizen Talbot formally conveyed the schooner *Fair Play* to Citizen Reddick and conscientiously took care of all the legal details required for the transfer of registry of an American

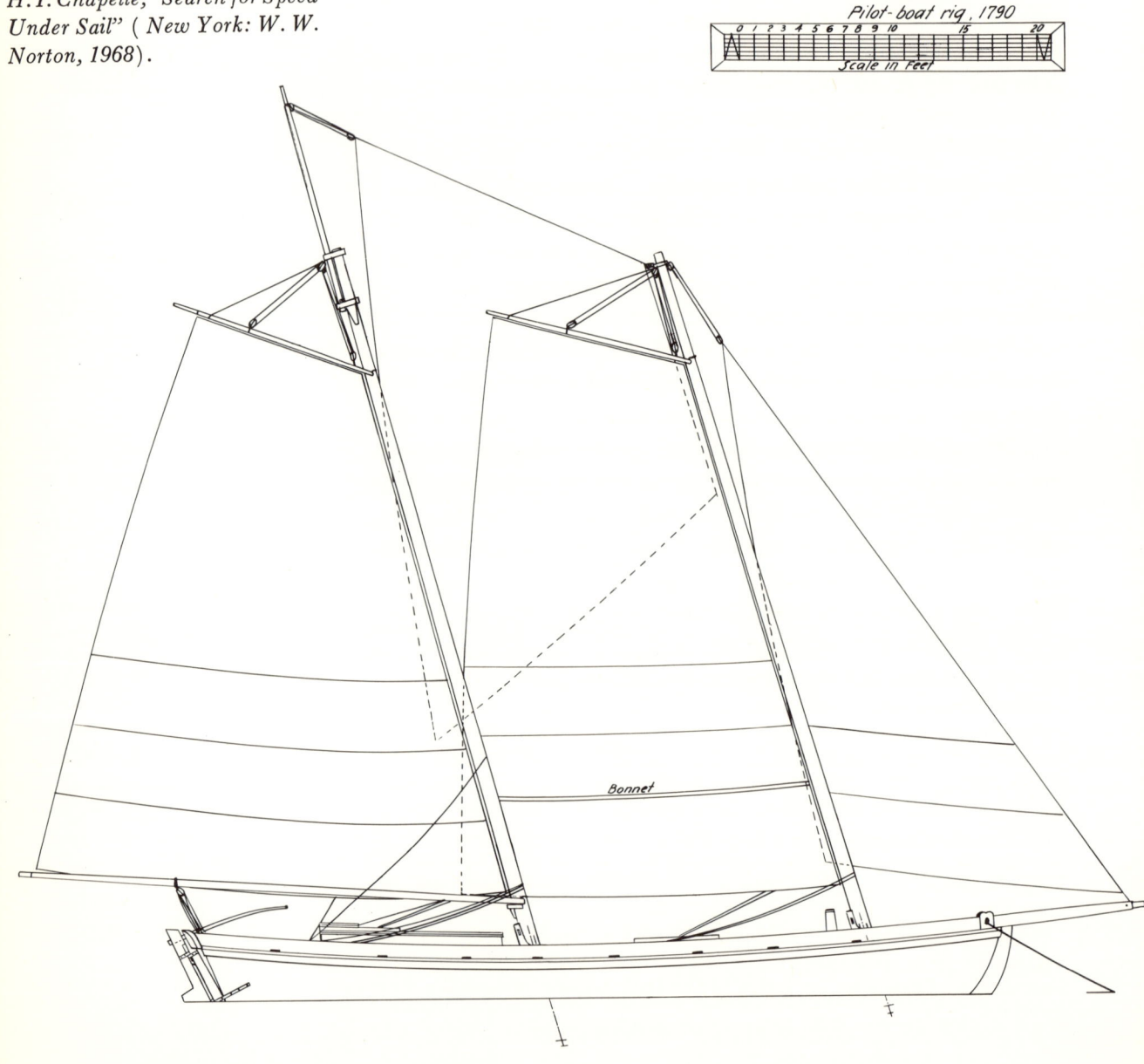

3 : THE WAY IS CLEARED

vessel. On January 2, 1794, the French armed schooner *l'Ami de la Pointe-à-Pitre* (ex-*Fair Play*) received her commission as a French privateer empowered "courrir sus les pirates, forbans, gens sans aveu et generalement sur tous les ennemis de la République française."

On the very day of commissioning, *l'Ami de la Pointe-à-Pitre* sailed on her first cruise.[15] A report from Saint Kitts also noted the sailing of the "American privateer" and commented:

> The example of the above vessel will, we apprehend, be followed by many other American vessels, in which case, Great Britain has no alternative and must of course declare war against the American States for having her subjects found in arms . . . .
>
> Thousands of Sans Culottes of America have long carried on war against England under the pretence of neutral trade, and now as their oaths, false papers, and other arts are detected, and that their vessels carrying French property cannot escape, we read and wonder at their recourse to French commissions, in order to plunder British subjects.[16]

By the time Talbot had appeared at Charleston to engage in the Florida expedition, he had captured nine prizes, and it was said that "British privateers of the Leeward Islands were afraid of meeting with him."

If the Florida expedition was a fiasco, Talbot nonetheless managed to bag an interesting prize, the British ship *Grenada Packet*, which he sent into Savannah before hurrying on to Charleston to keep his rendezvous with John Sinclair.[17] The reunion must have been joyous, and we may suspect that after division of the prize money accumulated by Talbot the usual privateersman's rout took place.[18] But the celebration was a short one, for Sinclair had developed new plans involving

---

[15] *Columbian Centinel*, February 24, 1794, news item datelined Basseterre, Guadeloupe, January 2, 1794: "An American privateer on the first inst. . . . The crew of the above privateer got naturalized and admitted French citizens."

[16] The *General Advertiser*, March 10, 1794.

[17] *The Grenada Packet*, Francis Hamilton, Pensacola for London, entered Savannah on April 19 (*Georgia Gazette*, April 24, 1794). The French consulate advertised her condemnation trial for April 25. Benjamin Moodie, in libelling the vessel, estimated her worth at £2,500 and her lading at £13,849/19/07 (BCC, Annex 2, pp. 616–617). However, before the vessel could be seized by the marshall she took fire from an overturned tar pot, floated up the river endangering wharfs and longshore property, burned to the water's edge, and sank. She was being fitted out for a privateer at the time she took fire. (*Georgia Gazette*, May 29, 1794).

[18] *Georgia Gazette*, May 1, 1794, dateline Charleston, April 28: "We learn from Captain Thomson of the *Carolina* of the transfer of accumulated prize money from Savannah to Charleston via inland water way, because of prowling British privateers."

the schooner *l'Ami de la Liberté* in which he had come to Charleston.[19]

Sinclair's acquisition of this vessel dated from the arrival of Admiral Jean Van Stabel's French squadron at Norfolk in January 1794 and the assembling of merchant vessels, both French and American under French charter, at the rendezvous in Hampton Roads. One of Van Stabel's major problems was the supression of intelligence leaks to the British on the state of forwardness of the great grain convoy. In order to prevent the British from fitting out dispatch boats to alert the British Admiralty it was necessary to keep the area under close surveillance; but with the embargo threatening in March and the stepped-up movement of shipping toward Hampton Roads, security became ever more difficult to maintain. Van Stabel began to charter ships to serve a dual role as tenders and guardships cruising the roadstead and its vicinity to keep watch on British shipping—especially on HMS *Daedalus,* whose presence there was particularly galling to the French. Taking advantage of this opportunity offered by Admiral Van Stabel, Sinclair and his partners had acquired a schooner which they named *l'Ami de la Liberté* and on April 3, 1794, procured from him what Sinclair later referred to as a "commission." *La Liberté,* as she will be called for the sake of brevity, was described as "raised from a pilot boat." Fitted with a railing and stanchions and a strake above the planksheer, she apparently had carried some armament when on duty with the French squadron, but upon her entry at Charleston she was noted as being unarmed.[20]

Between April 3 and 15, Sinclair hired Edward Ballard as captain but continued to remain on board as either passenger or supercargo. During the remainder of the time the French convoy was at Hampton Roads, Sinclair's vessel had served, under Van Stabel's charter, as one of several tenders functioning as the Admiral's unofficial embargo enforcement agents.[21] When the convoy moved to sea, Sinclair had accompanied it, secure in the knowledge that his "commission" would get him through the embargo. Once clear of the reach of Federal au-

---

[19] As were so many other vessels, this one was variously recorded, being *Amour de la Liberté*, *Friends of Liberty*, and variations of these names.

[20] BEE, *Reports*, p. 51, *Peter Martins* v. *Edward Ballard & William Talbot*.

[21] Sinclair was involved in the "unrigging and prevention of sailing of certain vessels," undoubtedly advice boats bought by the British at Norfolk to warn the British fleet of the convoy's sailing.

thority, *la Liberté* parted company with the convoy and headed south. The wind must have been fair and the schooner fast, for on April 20 she crossed the bar into Charleston harbor and there was duly entered at the customhouse as "not in distress, not armed: the embargo then in existence." [22]

Once at Charleston, Sinclair let it be known that he was on a "secret mission" entrusted to him by Admiral Van Stabel. But the appearance of Talbot and his impressive prize *Grenada Packet* made it important for Sinclair to remain ashore, and this need raised the problem of how to get *la Liberté* to sea under Ballard, as the "commission" was made out in Sinclair's name. Pleading his inability to command the schooner because of illness, Sinclair prevailed on Citizen Fonspertuis to endorse his "commission" over to Ballard. The consul was either completely bamboozled by the so-called commission or chose to close his eyes to what must have been obvious. The latter is probably nearer the truth.[23] On May 3, 1794, the consul's office applied for clearance for *la Liberté* and on May 5 the schooner sailed on her "secret mission of importance," followed closely by Talbot in *la Pointe-à-Pitre*. Ballard took *la Liberté* to Savannah, where he embarked guns and ammunition brought to him by Talbot, after which the two vessels set out to cruise in company.

While off the coast of Cuba, between May 15 and May 18, the two raiders ran across several strays from a British convoy bound for Europe. Separating, *la Pointe-à-Pitre* picked up the British brig *Elizabeth,* and on May 16 *la Liberté* overhauled the Dutch brigantine *Vrouw Christina Magdalena*. Ballard placed a prize crew on board the Hollander and the two continued in company. On the same day *la Pointe-à-Pitre* came up with *la Liberté* and her prize, and Captain Talbot placed an additional prize crew of his own on board *Magdalena*. On the next day another Dutch prize was taken, the *Fortuijn der Zee*, and both privateers placed crew members on board. Shortly after *Fortuijn* was seized, a strange sail was sighted and Talbot hastily removed *la Liberté's* men from both prizes leaving just his own men in possession. When the danger had passed *la Liberté's* men were again returned to the prizes.

---

[22] Bee, *Reports*, p. 267, *Joost Jansen* v. *The Brigantine Vrouw Christina Magdalene*
[23] Justice Bee later took Fonspertuis to task for his irregularity, laying it to either ignorance or a desire to rid himself of importuning applicants (Bee, *Reports*, p. 24).

It is not known whether any other prizes were taken on this joint cruise but the four vessels proceeded toward Charleston, remaining in company until two days before making port. *Elizabeth* was sent into Savannah, while *Vrouw Christina Magdalena,* along with *la Pointe-à Pitre* and *Fortuijn,* arrived at Charleston on May 25, followed shortly by *la Liberté.*

Dispensing with the formalities of condemnation, and with little regard for the law, Ballard at once set about converting the prizes into cash. Hatches were opened, cargo landed, bales and packages made free with, and ship's stores appropriated. He would have sold *Vrouw Christina Magdalena,* ship and cargo complete, had not the District Court of South Carolina intervened in response to a libel filed against the brigantine by her master Joost Janson. In demanding restitution and damages, the libelants alleged that the capture and sending in of *Magdalena* constituted a breach of the treaty between the United Netherlands and the United States. They further claimed that Ballard "was and is" a United States citizen and that *l'Ami de la Liberté* "was and is" an American vessel. Ballard, the libel asserted, did not have and could not have a French commission. Ballard, however, was much too busy in further forays against the "enemy" to answer the court's monitions, and after a third and last summons had been issued for him to appear, the libelants were awarded a default judgment.

On July 16, 1794, Ballard returned to port and the *City Gazette* reported the arrival of "the French schooner of war *Friends to Liberty.*"[24] It is interesting to note that she was still referred to as "a tender to the French Admiral Vanstabel [sic] who sent her on a particular mission." The cruise had been a good one, for *la Liberté* had captured the British sloop *Rambler* and two Spanish sloops, *la Santa Caterina,* from Saint Augustine for Havana, and *la Juno,* which arrived on July 16.[25]

When Ballard came ashore he was hit by a deluge of suits. Libels were filed against *Rambler* and, shortly after, against the Spanish prizes. In the main the respondents' allegations were the same as those in the *Magdalena* case. Again Ballard chose not to appear when summoned. In his stead appeared the privateer agent Abraham Sasportas, who, conceivably count-

---

[24] It must be noted (see footnote 19) that *l'Ami de la Liberté* was also referred to as "the French National Schooner" (*The City Gazette,* July 28, 1794).

[25] *City Gazette,* July 12, and July 17, 1794.

ing on the weight of Judge Bee's decision denying the jurisdiction of the U.S. courts in the case of *Castello* v. *Bouteille,* maintained that neither he nor Ballard was bound to appear or to answer the libel on the grounds that *l'Ami de la Liberté* was a French vessel, "fitted, armed, and commissioned by their [i.e., French]authority," and that Ballard was a French citizen.

Sasportas then made a grave error. He said that even if Ballard were not a French citizen he would still have the right to command a French vessel. Judge Bee would have none of this. He found Sasportas not only incompetent to appear in behalf of Ballard, who was then in contempt, but assessed costs against the agent as well. Yet as late as July 25 Ballard, to all appearances, was quite unconcerned by what was building up in the District Court. On that day, we learn, Citizen Edward Ballard, emulating the genial Jean Bouteille, was tendering "to a number of respectable citizens" a feast at Harris' Hotel where it was reported that no fewer than 15 patriotic toasts were offered to memorialize the glories of the two republics.

Ballard might have continued his career as a commander of a properly commissioned French privateer had not Captain Talbot sought to salvage what he could from the shambles that Ballard had made of the partnership's prospects. "As a French citizen acting under a commission from the Governor of Guadeloupe," he interposed his own claim as well as those of the owners, officers, and seamen of *l'Ami de la Pointe-à-Pitre*. But the ensuing trial succeeded only in disclosing further interesting facts regarding the operations of Talbot, Ballard, and Sinclair.

Ballard, of course, was far from being a French citizen and the so-called "commission" under which he was operating was merely a charter party, that is, an agreement for the hire of his vessel, made between Sinclair and Admiral Van Stabel. As a commission it was valueless. The shifting of crews between *la Liberté* and *la Pointe-à-Pitre* during and after the capture of *Magdalena* and *Fortuijn* was carried out to mask the fact that *la Liberté* was operating illegally. Indeed, such maneuvering was an old game with Captain Talbot. He had played it before with the "Spanish Launch" *San Joseph* which he had brought in with him at his first appearance in Charleston in April 1794.[26]

---

[26] Not to be confused with the *San Joseph* (*San José*) of the *Castello* v. *Bouteille* case (pp. 48–52), nor with the *San Joseph* captured by *la Montagne* off Saint Augustine on May 18 nor yet with the *St. Joseph* reported by Moodie (BCC, Moodie

San Joseph had been bought by Sinclair and Ballard for use as a raider and in some devious manner Governor Moultrie was induced to intercede with Federal officials to release the vessel from the embargo.

On April 13 *San Joseph*, mounting 3 guns and carrying a crew of 50, under the command of Captain Sweet, cleared Charleston for a cruise [27] and almost immediately fell in with the New Providence privateeer *Flying Fish,* mounting 12 6- and 4-pounders and manned by a crew of 56, under Captain McKenney. After a 15-minute engagement during which 4 men were killed, *San Joseph* struck her colors. The French privateer was sent off to Nassau and all but 15 of her men were loaded on board the British vessel *Speedwell* and sent back to Charleston, where they were set free on May 18.[28]

An examination of *San Joseph's* papers caused some very interesting information to come into the hands of British Consul Benjamin Moodie, who, in the cause of justice, handed it over to his Dutch allies, the libelants of *Vrouw Christina Magdalena*. *San Joseph,* the evidence revealed, had been cruising illegally under one of *la Pointe-à-Pitre's* prize passes at the time of her capture by *Flying Fish*. On August 9, *The City Gazette* announced the "decree of the long contested case of the Dutch Brigantine *Vrouw Christina Magdalena*." The facts of fraud were so strong that Judge Bee pronounced Talbot's plea to jurisdiction as irrelevant and decreed the restitution of vessel and cargo.[29]

It still remains to account for the fate of the ship *Elizabeth,* the first vessel captured by *la Pointe-à-Pitre* and *la Liberté*. This vessel, after her capture, made for Savannah, where her arrival with a cargo of 285 hogsheads of sugar, 90 puncheons of rum,

---

to Bond, December 17, 1794, p. 593) as a "handsome new Baltimore schooner cleared out for Port-de-Paix as a Spanish prize."

[27] Early in March 1795 Captain Sweet appeared as master of the privateer *Ça Ira* (see *City Gazette*, March 7, 1795).

[28] This incident is treated at some length in the *Georgia Gazette*, May 22, 1794, under the dateline of Charleston, May 19.

[29] Talbot appealed the case and it eventually went to the Supreme Court of the United States (reported in 3 Dallas 133). There the original claim was vastly overshadowed by the question of whether an American citizen had the right to expatriate himself, a constitutional question that loomed large in the last days of the 18th century. *Vrouw Christina Magdalena* and her cargo had to be offered for sale and the proceeds were held in escrow pending the final disposition of the case.

and 7 tons of fustic [30] was reported on May 22 in the *Georgia Gazette*. Once she was at anchor, the privateer's agents Messrs. Hills, May, and Woodbridge took charge of ship and cargo and proceeded to convert both to their own profit, and through "a fictitious and clandestine sale, [they] did themselves become the pretended purchasers . . . without having the same legally adjudicated, condemned or without forms or processes in the law." [31] Not until after the *Vrouw Christina Magdalena* case had been adjudged did Moodie decide to act against the seizure of *Elizabeth*. The libel was entered in October and, finally, on December 25 [32] the court decision was handed down. *Elizabeth* was to be returned to her owners and damages were assessed against all concerned in the affair.[33]

The career of *l'Ami de la Pointe-à-Pitre* did not end at this point, although it appears that Talbot no longer commanded her when she arrived at Charleston on October 15, 1794, from a cruise [34] during which she captured the British brig *Somerset*. This vessel, which had been sent into Savannah, was quickly libeled [35] and the same court that heard the *Elizabeth* case returned *Somerset* to her owners with damages.[36] *La Pointe-à-Pitre* sailed on yet another cruise and was next heard from in the vicinity of the Bahamas, where she took the British schooner *George*.[37] From a news item datelined Falmouth, Jamaica,[38]

---

[30] A dye-wood (*chlorophara tinctoria*) native of the West Indies, used to produce a yellow dye.

[31] In the *Georgia Gazette*, October 16, 1794, the text of the libel is printed in full.

[32] Although the case was scheduled to be heard at Augusta on November 2, the illness of the presiding judge caused a postponement until December and the jurisdiction was changed to Savannah.

[33] On January 22, 1795, the *Georgia Gazette* carried an advertisement announcing the sale of *Elizabeth* and her cargo by order of the "Admiralty Court." The sale was scheduled for February 10, 1795.

[34] The *City Gazette*, October 16, 1794, carried a garbled name, "Defanamyre," for her master.

[35] The *Georgia Gazette*, November 6, 1794, published a copy of the libel which named both Talbot and Ballard as being involved in the "piratical seizure."

[36] The *Georgia Gazette* of January 22 carried an advertisement for the sale of *Somerset* and her cargo to be held on February 10, 1795. Both the *Elizabeth* and *Somerset* decisions were appealed to the Circuit Court, and on May 4 that court reaffirmed the decision of the lower court (*Georgia Gazette*, May 7, 1795).

[37] *Georgia Gazette*, March 26, 1795. An article datelined Nassau, New Providence, stated that four seamen showed up at Nassau in a small boat, claiming to be part of the crew of *George* lately captured by "Pointe-à-Pitre, 10 guns, 47 men owned in Charleston." Actually, the four men were part of the privateer's prize crew, and were turned out of *George* when her crew rose and reseized the ship.

[38] *Georgia Gazette*, April 2, 1795.

we learn of an engagement between *la Pointe-à-Pitre* and the brig *Neptune,* presumably an American vessel, on January 8 off the west end of Tortuga. *Neptune* was ordered to Port-de-Paix in Saint Domingue, where her cargo was subjected to the type of forced sale that had become a standard procedure of the French colonial governments and one of growing concern to American merchants. Thereafter *l'Ami de la Pointe-à-Pitre* vanished under that name. Reappearing at Charleston as *l'Egalité,* commanded successively by Captains Pelletier, Pecheu, and De Latre, she operated with indifferent success until the end of 1795.[39]

Privateersman Edward Ballard paid dearly for his transgressions, not only for his participation in the capture of *Fortuijn der Zee* but for the seizing of his other prizes as well. If he escaped trial for piracy, his career was just as effectively halted by his confinement in debtor's prison. Even the sale of *l'Ami de la Liberté,* if its proceeds were indeed used to help him, could not meet the damages assessed against him.[40]

Sinclair left Charleston for Norfolk at about the time that Ballard and Talbot fell afoul of the law, and in July 1794 was again busily engaged in fitting out privateers. The last we hear of Sinclair is that one of his vessels, the *Smithfield,* was seized after an information was lodged against her by the resident agent of the United Netherlands, Van Berkel. When Sinclair tried to break his vessel out of detention, she was invested by militia and in November 1794 was finally dismantled.[41]

---

[39] Actually, *la Pointe-à-Pitre* seems to have come under new ownership while at Port-de-Paix. On February 25 the schooner *Egalité* entered Charleston and the *City Gazette* noted that she had captured no less than 19 prizes on her cruise (*City Gazette,* February 26, 1794). One of these, the brig *Everton* was sent into Savannah, where a libel was brought by the British consul and his agent John Wallace. The *Everton* was noted as having been captured on December 21, and that in addition to her cargo, £3,000 sterling had been taken from the prize. The libel stated that *l'Egalité* and *la Pointe-à-Pitre* were one and the same vessel. The court acted quickly on the libel. At the beginning of March *Everton* was returned to her owners. An appeal heard in May 1795, reaffirmed the decision of the lower court.

[40] After some years Ballard applied for relief under an act of Congress for the relief of insolvent debtors. Judge Bee, who heard the plea remorselessly refused on the grounds that Ballard's situation arose from the contravention of the treaty with the Netherlands and not from any civil cause recognized by the act.

[41] Miscellaneous Letters, 1789–1906, U.S. Department of State, Attorney for Virginia to the Secretary of State, July 11, 13, 16, 29, November 27, 1794.

Chapter 4

THE PALATINATE CHALLENGES UNITED STATES NEUTRALITY

A NASSAU NEWSPAPER NOTED AT THE END OF MAY 1794 that more than 12 privateers, fitted out and commissioned at Charleston, were enjoying considerable success in capturing English and Spanish prizes, and somewhat anxiously observed:

> Now that the situation of Affairs in the West Indies can admit of a part of the naval force in that quarter being detached on other service, we trust the depredations on the British trade committed by these French American privateers, will be one of the first objects to attract the attention of our Admirals.[1]

But the breathing spell for the British in the West Indies was too short to admit of detaching the hoped-for force. On June 2, just when they seemed to have gained control of the Caribbean and, according to the Reverend Bentley, a rush of shipping was clearing United States ports to take advantage of West Indies trade prospects, a small French expeditionary force under Représentant en Mission Victor Hugues had stormed ashore at Gosier on Guadeloupe's Grandeterre. The British garrison, plagued by fever, and its high command demoralized by bickering and indecision, was outmaneuvered, outfought, and cut to pieces by the savagery of the French attack.

Before the rubble of Pointe-à-Pitre stopped smouldering, Hugues began to rebuild a French stronghold in the Caribbean.

---

[1] According to the *City Gazette*, July 1, 1794, in a story datelined Nassau, New Providence, May 27.

For this effort naval and merchant shipping were essential. But except for the two frigates and three transports that had landed his force at Guadeloupe, not a single French naval unit above the rating of a corvette was to be found in the Caribbean, and the British control of the Lesser Antilles had eliminated French merchant shipping there.

Here it must be recalled that when the great French grain fleet left the Chesapeake in April 1794, France had ordered every available man-of-war to sea to meet and escort the convoy through the British blockade. Although the convoy successfully reached France, the sea battle (known as the Glorious First of June) between a British fleet seeking to intercept the convoy and the French covering force resulted in a crippling blow to France's naval power which took many years to repair. Thereafter France had to husband her strength for the multifarious demands in French home waters, and especially to mount offensives against England. Naval needs of colonial areas were perforce unheeded and so it was that Victor Hugues could count on little aid beyond the infrequent appearance of French naval units on special missions.

Compelled to build his own striking force, he fell back on the classic solution of Caribbean sea warfare, the privateer. The ships necessary to supply the French stronghold were assembled by the simple expedient of capturing British merchantmen. The cargoes of such prizes met his immediate needs for supplies and weapons, while surplus cargoes thus obtained were traded off to neutrals for additional supplies. Prizes suitable for privateering were quickly commissioned and sent out on cruises.

Hugues' successful assault on Guadeloupe and the energy with which he exploited his opportunities was directly responsible for saving Saint Domingue from complete collapse. And within six months of the French landings there he had set up a system of agencies in the neutral Swedish and Danish islands that was later to be expanded to the leading ports of the United States. The British, again faced with an active French base in the heart of the lesser Antilles, were forced to abandon the *coup-de-grâce* they had prepared as a follow-up to their capture of Port-au-Prince on June 5.

Meanwhile, the French area commanders on Saint Domingue, relieved from immediate threat of invasion and, coincidentally, from the meddling of the commissioners Sonthonax and Polverel (who had been recalled to answer to charges of maladministration), managed to iron out their differences for a short time. General Etienne Laveaux was named Governor ad interim of Saint Domingue and supreme commander of French forces in the colony. Together with Toussaint l'Overture, whom Laveaux wooed away from his alliance with the Spanish and whom he had made commandant of the Western Cordon, Laveaux succeeded in bringing a degree of stability to the northern part of Saint Domingue. The capture of Jean Rabel in April 1794, and offensive actions against the Spanish invaders had been followed by the clearing away of much of the ruins in the vicinity of Grande Rivière and the reinstitution of a semblance of the old plantation economy. Laveaux like Hugues, was in desperate need of supplies of all kinds to carry out operations against the Spanish and the British by land, and he turned to Charleston as a principal source of supply for food,

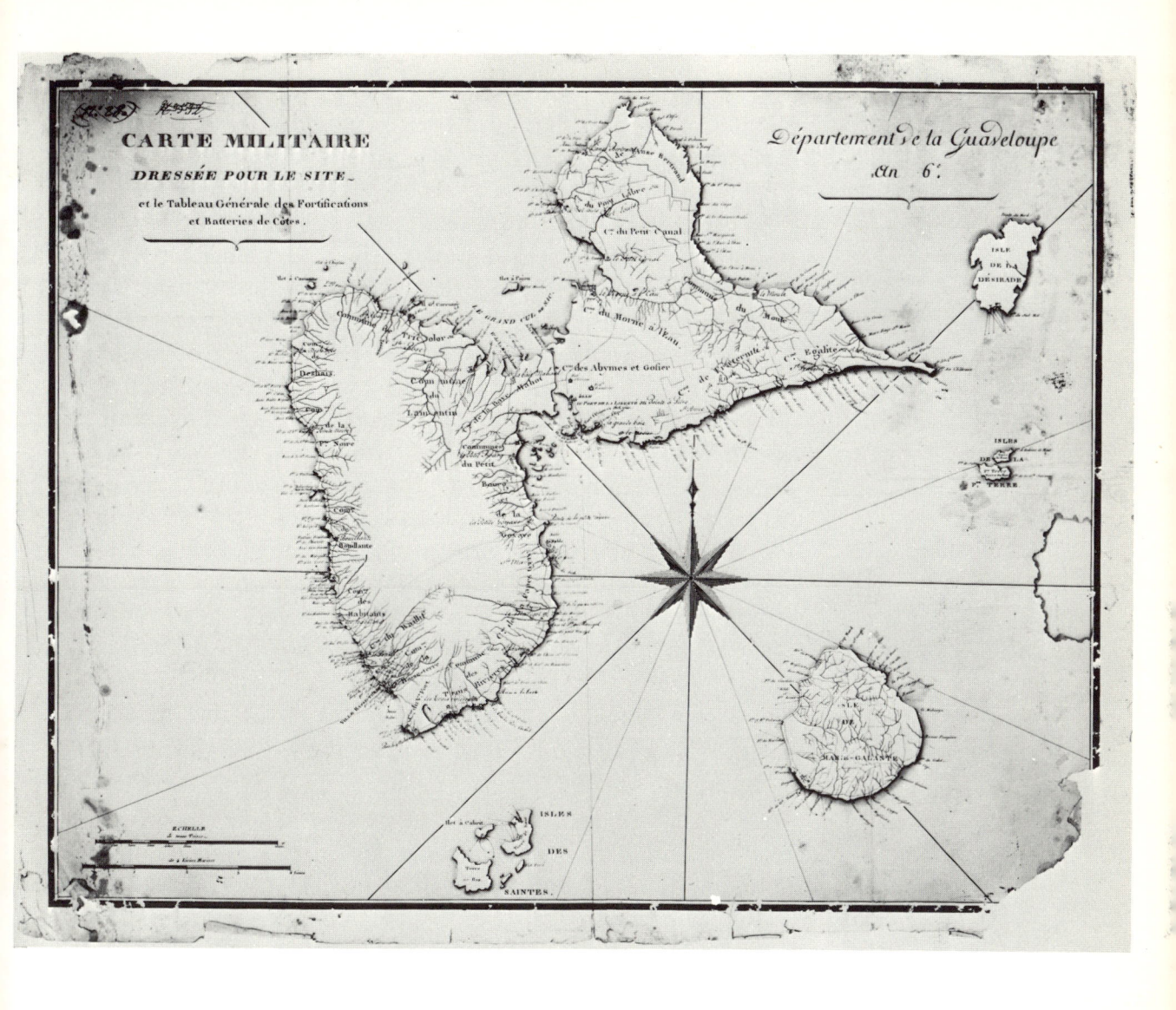

Manuscript map, 1797–1798, of "Département de la Guadeloupe, An 6ᵉ. Carte Militaire dressée pour le site et le Tableau Générale des Fortifications et Batteries de Côtes." From Archives de France Outre-Mer, Paris, transferred to Archives Nationales.

munitions, and also that most essential element, the bottoms to carry the cargoes as well as to strike out offensively against France's enemies at sea.

In Charleston, Laveaux's appeal for aid, supported by the organizing ability of vice-consul Fonspertuis, called forth an enthusiastic response from privateersmen, outfitters, and the sizable membership of the democratic societies. By midsummer 1794 an organization known as the Council for the Republic made its appearance under the leadership of the consul and had assumed the role of agency for the collection and forwarding of supplies of all descriptions to Port-de-Paix.[2] Laveaux, impressed by the importance of the Council to his war effort, sent his personal representative Préssinet as deputy and adviser to aid Fonspertuis. The latter in turn sent Préssinet to Philadelphia to make a first-hand report to Minister Fauchet on the state of affairs in Saint Domingue. This resulted in an emergency shipment of 1,600 barrels of flour to replenish the exhausted warehouses of the colony, and Philadelphia and Baltimore agents and merchants soon thereafter extended credits for further shipments of provisions.[3] But as important as were foodstuffs to the renewed effort of the French in the West Indies, even more essential were the munitions of war—cannon, powder, muskets, and shot. And most essential was the need for fast-sailing, well-armed vessels, for, as Victor Hugues had demonstrated, by means of them the other essentials could be summoned into existence.

It was the endeavor to clear out shipments of arms and vessels to the resurgent French in the West Indies that brought about a new confrontation between United States national policy and French imperatives in the Caribbean.

The war tension in the United States that marked the period from January to May 1794 had revealed, as the country was canvassed for contractors able to supply cannon, shot and shell, and

---

[2] *Le Moniteur Universel*, June 5, 1795, quotes a letter from Roger, aide-de-camp of General Laveaux to Préssinet, deputy to the consul at Charleston, that refers to Préssinet's activities at Charleston and his visit to Philadelphia and also to a visit to Port-de-Paix by "le digne républicain" Carvin, and that notes the receipt of Fauchet's shipment of flour. By context the letter may be dated between the middle of July and middle of August. Except for this reference, no further information about the Council for the Republic has been found in contemporary newspapers, but it may be supposed that the Council was an organ of the Republican Society.

[3] CABON, *Histoire de Haiti*, vol. 4, pp. 118–122.

ship timbers, an appalling lack of any of these essentials of national defense. Consequently, measures were undertaken to conserve what arms were in existence and to encourage the importation of the raw materials needed to put the country's defenses in some semblance of readiness. One such measure was the Act of May 22, 1794, that placed a one-year embargo on the export of cannon, muskets, pistols, bayonets, cutlasses—in short, on the entire range of arms and armament. An exception was made for the arming of vessels, but if the value of such an armament exceeded 400 dollars, the articles were to be forfeited and the vessel subject to seizure.[4]

This Act was followed on June 4 by another titled "An Act in Addition to the Act for the Punishment of Certain Crimes against the United States,"[5] which, although primarily aimed at closing the loopholes in the Neutrality Act discovered and used by those fitting out belligerent privateers in American ports, also reinforced the decisions of the Supreme Court rendered at the beginning of 1794 and neatly complemented the Act of May 22. It clearly stated that fitting out a vessel or procuring one to be fitted out or the issuance of a commission to one within the jurisdiction of the United States for the purpose of privateering was to be punishable by the forfeiture of the vessel concerned, a fine of 5,000 dollars, and a jail term of three years. It further stipulated that any increase or augmentation of armament was unlawful, as was adding to the number and size of the guns, or the addition of equipment "solely applicable to war."

On July 22 *The City Gazette* quoted for the benefit of readers who might be interested what was meant by "augmentation of armament" according to the Secretary of War:

> The mounting of additional guns, or changing or altering the calibre of guns in any manner whatever; the making of new gun carriages, or the cutting of new portholes in any part of the vessel, are adjudged to be unlawful augmentation of force, and is therefore to be prevented.

Much as these Acts hindered the French in their acquisition of weapons for the colonial war effort—this at a time when the tide of British success in the Caribbean seemed to have been halted—a regulation of the Secretary of War, at first not fully appreciated, posed an even greater obstacle to exporting fully armed vessels:

---

[4] *U.S. Statutes at Large*, chapt. 32.
[5] Ibid., chapt. 50.

The United States being a neutral nation, the vessels of their citizens, in most cases do not require to be armed. To guard against any abuse, no vessel belonging to any citizen of the United States is to be permitted to be armed and sail until after all circumstances concerning her shall have been transmitted to the President and his decision thereon be made known.[6]

This restrictive legislation and the regulations imposed by the Federal Government were met by redoubled ingenuity on the part of Charleston privateering entrepreneurs and arms exporters seeking to evade them. In this, they were aided by conveniently near-sighted officials and by merchants resentful of interference in a lucrative trade. British Minister Hammond, writing in 1896, alluded to that resentment as basic to the Government's lack of success in preventing the outfitting of French privateers:

Indeed, Mr. Chase, one of the Federal judges, gave it as his opinion that the citizens of the United States had a right to build and equip ships of war as an article of trade, and to dispose of them to either belligerent powers without any breach of neutrality, provided that none of them were in any manner concerned in them after they became cruisers.[7]

The evasions devised by the privateersmen were many, of which some are revealed in the correspondence of British consul Benjamin Moodie and in records of the lawsuits he instituted.

One means of procuring armed vessels, as we have seen, was to capture the enemy's armed shipping. These vessels could be made available for the Caribbean war effort with minimum delay, provided that no attempt was made to alter them in a manner conflicting with the new United States Government regulations, and also provided that the captor's legal position was in good order.

The latter provision was very often a real obstacle, however, for the pedigrees of French privateers were closely scrutinized by the British consul and his agents as well as by the agents of His Catholic Majesty. Because so many of the French commissions were of doubtful validity, the predilection was strong for consular officials, masters, and supercargoes to interpose "shotgun" libels against prizes based on a claim of illegal capture. Also a fertile ground for libels were the still largely uninterpreted treaties entered into between the United States and the sovereign of the country of origin of the captured vessel. Prizes libeled on this basis could be tied up over an extended

---

[6] *The City Gazette*, July 22, 1794.
[7] BCC, p. 607.

period pending litigation, and many appeals were taken as far as the Supreme Court. Benjamin Moodie, for his part, undertook to enter libels against prizes brought in by French raiders as a policy of harassment, without regard to the fact that penalties were often assessed for failure to make an adequate case.

Another and generally preferred means of acquiring armed vessels was to purchase ships of American registry already armed, such as those that had been set up in American yards as privateers when war with England was threatening. Tapping this source of supply had its risks, especially after promulgation of the Acts of May and June 1794, but the number of ready-built American vessels equipped as raiders was such that a brisk market was open to the privateer entrepreneur and exporter. A notable example of such a sale was the new brig *Pulaski,* built by the New York yard of Rivington for the Charleston firm of Cross and Crawley, which arrived at Charleston on November 24, 1794, and was immediately put up for sale.[8] This "remarkably fine vessel" as Moodie termed her, was "sold to some Frenchmen for 18,000 dollars." She presumably needed little if any work done to her and after several metamorphoses, as noted below, she reappeared as the French National vessel *le Brutus Français,* (ex- *le Pichegru,* see p. 84).[9] The majority of vessels, however, whether bought or captured, needed refitting in some degree to ready them for cruising, and hence their owners tended to become entangled in United States laws.

The history of the privateer brig *le Général Laveaux* illustrates the procedures and some of the complications that developed in fitting out purchased privateers.

This raider started life as the American brig *Cygnet.* As was true of the *Pulaski* she had been laid down as a privateer during the war scare.[10] She was purchased by the privateer agent and local merchant Abraham Sasportas and Jean Gaillard,[11] a former chief officer in Carvin's *l'Industrie.* Between the middle

---

[8] *The City Gazette*, November 24, 1794.

[9] Moodie provides this identification in his letter to Phineas Bond dated December 17, 1794 (see BCC, p. 601).

[10] Unless otherwise noted, information pertaining to *le Général Laveaux* is derived from *British Consul* v. *ship Mermaid* in Bee, *Reports,* pp. 69–73.

[11] Not connected with the Charleston family of the same name that owned the wharf where much of the ship conversion took place. A brief biography of the man appears in Théric's Memorial.

of May and the end of June 1794, Sasportas personally directed the work of fitting her out. This entailed, in essence, a reconversion to her warlike origin, rather than the conversion of a merchant ship into a warship, for her original gun ports had been "nailed up and caulked in" outboard, while inboard over the stanchions a ceiling had been installed which effectively masked the ports from view. (It was later stressed, however, that from outboard the old gun ports were clearly defined.) The partners ripped off the inboard ceiling and the outboard planking, and opened her old ports as they had been built. Her quarter deck was removed and "rotted timbers and planks were replaced."[12]

Moodie watched the proceedings carefully and kept the collector of customs advised. In return he was assured that the vessel would be detained. At about the time the embargo ended, *Cygnet* was reported to have been sold to one Ladevize, an American citizen. With her name changed to *le Général Laveaux*, her clearance for Port-de-Paix was sought. At this point the collector of customs seized the vessel. She was subjected to an intensive examination, her guns were landed, and her hold was searched for "warlike instruments." Nothing was found, but the new owner was forced to reseal the recently opened gun ports, after which, with no further grounds for detention and over Moodie's protest, *le Général Laveaux* (ex-*Cygnet*) was allowed to go to sea, since she made no pretentions to being a privateer. If Moodie is to be believed, *le Général Laveaux*'s guns were somehow repossessed and sent out to be loaded on board the brig when she had cleared the bar. The lightering service was performed by none other than William Talbot in *l'Ami de la Pointe-à-Pitre*.[13] Every indication points to the fact that *le Général Laveaux* proceeded to Port-de-Paix and there picked up her commission; in subsequent court proceedings no question was raised as to its validity.

Upon her return to Charleston, accompanied by the British prize *Mermaid,* the legality of her outfitting was tested by a libel filed by the British consul. In the ensuing trial Judge Bee

---

[12] The fact that the vessel contained bad timber although she could not have been above six months old at the time presents an interesting commentary on the quality of material employed in order to get a privateer to sea in the shortest possible time when war threatened.

[13] See p. 57, above, on the arming of *l'Ami de la Liberté* (BCC, Moodie to Miller, November 28, 1794, p. 600).

heard "various and contradictory evidence" much of which, he said, he would have rejected if both parties had not "intimated an intention to appeal." The libel charged that *le Général Laveaux* was a French vessel when she sailed from Charleston; that she was fitted out for war in Charleston and that her crew, for the most part, was American. The respondents Sasportas and Gaillard [14] denied the libel in all its points. Any question about the legality of the transfer of *le Général Laveaux*'s registry was quickly resolved when the respondents produced a bill of sale and testimony from the collector of the customs which acknowledged that the ship's register had been delivered up legally and that *Cygnet*'s bond was duly surrendered with the change of nationality of the vessel.

Ship Recovery *built by Retire Becket for E. H. Derby in 1794 for use in the East Indies trade. Vessels like this were much sought by the French because little alteration was required to make them powerful privateers. She could have carried 18 guns. Courtesy the Peabody Museum of Salem, Massachusetts.*

---

[14] The fact that Sasportas and Gaillard answered the libel seems at first to give point to Moodie's charge that the sale of *Cygnet* had been rigged (BCC, Moodie, to Bond, April 28, 1795, p. 602).

The work on *le Général Laveaux* was readily admitted, but the respondents maintained that it was not illegal: the vessel had been originally built as a private ship of war in anticipation of hostilities with Great Britain, and she was merely being restored to her original condition rather than in any sense being converted to a warship from a merchant ship. Was it then, illegal to arm the vessel? Bee decided it was not:

> The laws of neutrality and nations in no instance that I know of, interdict neutral vessels from going to sea armed and fitted out for defensive war. All American Indiamen are armed, and it is necessary that they be so![15]

Judge Bee's reasoning seems eminently clear when we recall that *Cygnet* was sold with her armament as part of her "furniture and equipment." Thus, as *le Général Laveaux* she retained every right to proceed to sea armed. In many respects the Secretary of Treasury's circular letter which had played such an important part in the release of Carvin's *l'Industrie* from detention at Baltimore a year earlier, again became pertinent. There could hardly have been a question of doubt as to whether *le Général Laveaux*'s armament was offensive or defensive, and hence the vessel could not be deprived of her ordnance.

The applicability of the two Acts of Congress, particularly that of June 5, 1794, was also assayed. The alteration and refitting of the vessel might have been made pertinent except that the work had been completed prior to the latter Act. The charge that the vessel was manned by Americans could not be substantiated over the denial of the respondents, for the bar pilot who took *le Général Laveaux* to sea testified that her crew of about 40 men "were all outlandish" and only one of them seemed to be able to speak English.

Alluding to the alleged infringement of the Act of May 22, Judge Bee considered that the action of the collector in searching the vessel, in taking off her armament, and in causing her ports to be restored to their former condition was itself sufficient. The vessel, after all, was still American and there could be no justification in rendering her useless to her owners. As for her being rearmed by *le Pointe-à-Pitre* outside the bar that evidence was held to be hearsay. Finally, since there was no question of the prize having been taken anywhere but on the high seas, Judge Bee dismissed the libel and levied costs against the libelants.

---

[15] BEE, *Reports*, p. 71.

Moodie raged against the decision. He complained of the depravity of witnesses who gave evidence "upon oath contrary to their own knowledge" and insinuated that Bee showed a distinct anti-British bias.[16] Although plagued by a shortage of funds to stoke his legal backfires, Moodie was aware that it was essential to appeal the decision of the District Court if the four other prizes made by *le Général Laveaux* subsequent to the capture of *Mermaid* were to avoid the same fate.[17] He therefore wearily requested instructions as to whether he should proceed to the next higher court, scheduled to meet in Columbia, South Carolina on May 12. As for the ship *Phyn,* another of *le Général Laveaux*'s prizes, which had been sent into Charleston on February 26, 1795,[18] Moodie felt she was not even worth libeling if they were not ready to take her case to the Circuit Court as well: "We can expect little from the District Court."[19]

The fitting out of *le Général Laveaux* was only one of many such operations. They followed the same general pattern, but some of the variations are of interest.

The *San José,* the same vessel that was captured by Jean Bouteille and was featured in the trial *Castello* v. *Bouteille et al.,* was also fitted out for a raider. The *San José*'s rig was altered while she was alongside a wharf and when all was ready she was warped out into the harbor and anchored just within the bar. There, just prior to sailing, her quarter deck was razed, gunports cut in, and her guns mounted. Bouteille brought off the job without let or hindrance of the authorities.[20]

---

[16] BCC, p. 602, Moodie to Bond, April 28, 1795. In relating Judge Bee's summation of the evidence Moodie wrote, "The judge said previous to the promulgation of the law of June 5 . . . Sasportas or any other citizen of the United States, had a right to arm their vessels for self-defense, and that the general unanimity then prevailing . . . to obtain redress for depredations committed by the British on their trade had occasioned the arming all along the continent; and that in such instance the arming became meritorious, *and that had a war with Great Britain then taken place, he did not doubt but the British West India Trade would have received a mortal wound* [Italics supplied]."

[17] Among these were *Jamaica* and *la Tendre Mère* (apparently owned by French emigrés under British registry), captured in company with the Charleston-based privateer *la Mère Michel,* and *Tivoli*. All these vessels had been taken in February 1795 and sent into Charleston. *City Gazette*, February 10, 16, and March 26, 1795.

[18] A monition for the trial of the ship *Phya* [sic] appeared in the *City Gazette*, March 3, 1795. The date for the trial was set for March 12.

[19] Records of the final disposition of the *Mermaid* case have proved elusive. Newspaper notices indicate, however, that *le Général Laveaux* carried on operations well into 1796.

[20] BCC, p. 589, Moodie to Miller, November 28, 1794.

In another case the outfitters employed a bit more finesse in evading the Act of June 5, 1794. At the end of November a brigantine from Port-de-Paix, very possibly *le Port-de-Paix* (ex-*le Vulcan*, ex-*le Vainqueur de la Bastille*), was fitting out at Gaillard's wharf. This vessel was already pierced for 12 guns upon her arrival at Charleston. While alongside the wharf the bulkhead between her raised poop and waist was knocked out and deck beams were fitted from the old break aft to the counter, without affecting the raised poop. Once clear of the harbor the poop stanchions were sawn through at the height of her bulwarks and the structure was heaved overside. Presto! A fine flush-deck privateer. All that remained to be done was to sway on board her guns and take in her ammunition, all of which were lightered out to her.[21]

In the frantic search for armed vessels to meet the soaring demand even candidates for the "boneyard" did not escape the attention of the outfitters. One such was the ship *le Dauphin* of L'Orient which made her appearance at Charleston during the embargo and on May 20 was advertised for sale "for the benefit of the underwriters." At the auction which took place at Mey's wharf on July 23, 1794, she was bid in by Jean Bouteille for an undisclosed sum. A relic of the American War of Independence, she had been built for the Continental Congress as the frigate *Delaware,* and in 1777 was captured and entered into the Royal Navy. In 1788 she was sold out of the service to French South Sea whaling interests. What other trades she served during her 17-year life is not known.[22]

With a potential armament of 32 12-pounders and 6 6-pounders (her former establishment as a frigate was 24 guns) the vessel would have been a dangerous weapon in the hands of Etienne Laveaux, then exerting heavy pressure on Britain's Spanish ally.

Moodie worked hard to keep the old frigate from sailing and apparently enjoyed some success. In a memorial to the National Convention drawn up by "Les Capitaines & Armateurs des Corsairs Français en Rade de Charleston," dated "12 Nivose De L'an 3ᵉ [January 1, 1795]," complaint was made that al-

---

[21] Ibid., p. 591, December 14, 1794.

[22] For further information on *Delaware*, see H. I. Chapelle, *The History of the American Sailing Navy* (New York: Norton, 1949), pp. 75, 78, 90. See also advertisements in *The City Gazette*, May 20, June 4, July 21, 23, 1794: in the latter two she was identified as the former *Delaware;* her tonnage was given as 604.

4: PALATINATE CHALLENGES NEUTRALITY

though Captain Bouteille had been most scrupulous in abiding by the letter of the American law, *le Dauphin* had been placed in detention by "un ordre Arbitraire & Despotique arrivé de [President] Wasghinton [sic]." Bouteille, the memorial noted bitterly, had put all the profits from his successful *la Sans Pareille* into this patriotic venture which had been designed as a gift for General Laveaux.[23] Rehabilitation of *le Dauphin* proved to be long and costly but in March it was finally reported near completion.

Moodie, under orders to keep a careful tally of the comings and goings of the French raiders, more often than not was kept in a state of bewilderment by the manipulations of the privateersmen. On one occasion, in answering a request from Philadelphia on the whereabouts of a vessel called *la Signoria* (sic), he supposed that she had gone in one of Carvin's fleets to Saint Domingue:

> Truly, what with the increase in numbers and change of name, commissions, and masters, it is impossible to trace them; and still more so to obtain such particular information as Mr. Moore requires. Can he be aware of the partiality of the inhabitants, the number of privateers and that they neither enter inwards nor clear outward at the custom-house?[24]

At the time of Moodie's letter the Charleston-Saint Domingue shuttle was at its peak. Jean Bouteille and Jean Baptiste Carvin were in the forefront of the privateersmen who had come to the aid of their countrymen struggling against the British and Spanish in and around Saint Domingue by forwarding arms and munitions and by pressing the war along the sea lanes. Carvin's success at privateering is manifest in his sending to sea what amounted to a privately owned fleet to aid General Laveaux in a design against the Spanish stronghold of Montechristi on the north coast of Hispaniola.[25] Bouteille, not to be outdone by

---

[23] Théric in his Etat Nominatif listing the privateers based at Charleston appended a request that Bouteille be reimbursed and aided in bringing about the completion of the *Dauphin*. Since the Etat was written no later than May 1795, it seems more than likely that Bouteille had undertaken a job too big for his purse. The subsequent career of this vessel is not known with any degree of certainty.

[24] BCC, p. 592. Moodie's problem in identifying *La Signoria* may be better appreciated from the following culling of Spanish prizes sent into Charleston by French privateers during the period concerned (the spelling is that of the news paper notices): "*La Signiora de la - - - -*," "*Signora Candelero*," "*Signior de Car - - -*," "*La Sinteric*," "*La Seignorita*."

[25] See Théric, Memorial. The strike against Montechristi did not occur, because Carvin fell ill and Laveaux was reluctant to entrust the flotilla to any but Carvin's

his former partner, forwarded at his own expense both *provisions de bouche* and a variety of munitions to supply Laveaux's forces. Indeed, *la Signoria,* about which Moodie had been asked by his superior at Philadelphia, was one of Bouteille's vessels. Together with his *la Narbonnaise,* commanded by the ubiquitous Hervieux, it was part of one of the flotillas which carried an extremely valuable cargo of powder and arms to Port-de-Paix in the last half of November.

The provenance of the powder and the chain of events and complications which surrounded its dispatch to Saint Domingue constitute an episode difficult to equal for the number of facets it displays of French privateering operations out of Charleston.

The north coast of Cuba had been a favorite cruising ground of the French privateers since the outbreak of the war. Havana was the cynosure of Spanish colonial trade and at that port all cargoes were consolidated for the run to the Iberian Peninsula. This pattern of traffic was as old as the Spanish empire on Tierra Firme. Between June and December 1794 shipping began to converge on Havana from Caracas, Cartagena de las Indias, Vera Cruz, Campeche, Florida, Santo Domingo, and Puerto Rico, carrying royal treasure and private cargoes for the eastbound convoy.

In June, Don Gabriel Aristizabal, Lieutenant-General in command of Spain's naval forces in the Caribbean, set up his headquarters at Havana in order to repair and refit the escort force for the home-bound fleet. Plagued by epidemics of fever in the two squadrons based on Havana and by the devastation of one hurricane which struck on July 22 and another which played havoc with a fleet of merchantmen en route from Vera Cruz, Don Gabriel found himself seriously short of men, arms, munitions, and supplies of all kinds. To fill his desperate need he was forced to send out vessels to make levies on every possible source of supply in the Spanish Caribbean.[26]

Towards the end of September 1794 César Peronne, in command of Carvin's 12-gun sloop *le Républicain*, was cruising the heavily traveled approaches to Havana harbor. He had already taken several prizes when in quick succession, he came into

---

command. Théric notes that involved were *l'Industrie*, 12 guns; the brig *le Sans Culotte*, 14 guns; the sloop *le Républican;* and the schooner *la Carmagnole*, 16 guns.

[26] The details of Spanish naval movements at Havana are contained in "Extracto de las ocurencias diarios de la escuadra del mando de teniente general Don Gabriel Aristizabal . . . .," Museo Naval, Madrid, Ms. 595, Doc. 1.

possession of the British brig *Eagle,* a Letter of Marque of 14 guns, and the Spanish ship *la Trasmerana,* of 16 guns, from Vera Cruz for Havana.[27] Upon capturing *Eagle,* Peronne placed on board the British vessel a prize captain and half of *le Républicain*'s crew. The two vessels continued to cruise in company until September 19 when *la Trasmerana* was overhauled, boarded, and seized. Both prizes were ordered for Savannah where they arrived on September 29.[28]

The cargo of *la Trasmerana* was a veritable windfall consisting of peas, beans, lead, logwood, dried meat, and 842 150-

"A Bermudian sloop with a view upon the Spanish Main," three aspects of the same sloop in a West Indian harbor during the last half of the eighteenth century. Vessels of this type, a favored rig in American and Caribbean waters, often served as privateers. The size and weight of their gear, however, made them less desirable than the schooner.

---

[27] The account of the capture of these vessels is confused. Théric, possibly writing from memory in November 1795, gives the impression that it was Carvin himself who captured *Eagle* while in command of a new privateer called *le Vengeur*. However, Théric is alone in associating the capture of *Eagle* or *la Trasmerana* with *le Vengeur*. That vessel does not appear at Charleston until March 1795. Théric also mentions that Carvin had placed Joseph Langlois on board *Eagle* and that it was Langlois in turn who captured *la Trasmerana*. Langlois is not mentioned in the libels that were instituted against both vessels. (See Théric, Memorial, ff. 212v, 213.) Théric's account is also at variance with that contained in the memorial written by "Les Capitans & Armateurs des Corsaires Français en Rade de Charleston . . . 12 Nivose de l'an 3eme [January 2, 1795]."

[28] *Georgia Gazette*, October 2, 1794, announced the arrival of *Eagle* and *la Trasmerana* as prizes to *le Républicain*. The former was noted as mounting 12 guns, from Vera Cruz for Havana "with a cargo of guns, powder, and balls . . . ."

pound boxes of gunpowder, as well as 4,242 Spanish dollars in specie and the vessel's 12 cannon, of unidentified caliber.[29] Almost immediately upon arrival the privateersmen and their agent, Mordecai Sheftall, began with their usual dispatch to liquidate ship and cargo. It is not clear how much of the cargo was disposed of by the time that *la Trasmerana*'s master managed to lodge with the District Court of Georgia, a libel against his former vessel, but from an advertisement which appeared in the *City Gazette* on October 25, 1794, at least 1,400 pounds of it might have found its way to Charleston.

According to the libel, *la Trasmerana* was not seized by *le Républicain* but by the brig *Eagle*, and the presumption was that Peronne was playing William Talbot's game of fobbing off a prize pass as a legal commission. The latter vessel, it was maintained, had been fitted out at Charleston. The capture was therefore illegal and piratical, and restitution of ship and cargo and damages, were demanded. The libel was followed by seizure of the vessel, and such cargo as remained intact was impounded and duly moved off to a warehouse pending adjudication of the case. The attorney for the captors denied all the allegations in the libel, insisting that *la Trasmerana* was a good prize, made by *le Républicain,* a legally commissioned privateer sloop. As time went by and Peronne failed to show up, tempers began to flare. Privateersmen in both Savannah and Charleston saw in the delay attending the libel hearings on the precious cargo yet another instance of American ill will.[30]

Nine days later, on October 25, still another of *le Républicain's prizes, la Princesa de Asturias,* a 15-gun brig, entered the Thunderbolt River. The whereabouts of the French privateer was finally learned when, on the same day, the British frigate *Hussar,* 28 guns, and the sloop-of-war *Scorpion,* appeared off Charleston bar and announced that they had captured *le Républicain* as well as another small raider.[31]

---

[29] Details of her lading were printed in the libel cited by D. Pedro Trabudua (on November 17, 1794) and printed by the *Georgia Gazette*, December 4, 1794. Théric reported that *Las Tres Meronas* (sic) carried 900 chests of 300 pounds each of cannon powder (Memorial, f. 213), while "Les Capitaines & Armateurs" mentioned 105,000 pounds of powder as the lading of the vessel.

[30] The outraged "Capitaines & Armateurs" branded the proceeding as "un acte de rigeur et arbitraire en faveur de nos ennemis, les Espagnols."

[31] *The City Gazette*, October 25, 1794. On January 15, 1795, the *Georgia Gazette* published, under the dateline "Halifax, November 3, 1794" an account of the taking of *le Républicain,* "one of the best privateers which, for the disgrace of the

4: PALATINATE CHALLENGES NEUTRALITY

It is not certain when Captain Peronne reappeared on the scene; possibly he was one of the French seamen landed from *Hussar* on the evening of October 25.[32] Moodie gives the impression that Peronne was in Charleston on December 17, 1794, at the time he wrote his letter to Phineas Bond. He was not, however, one of those who signed the memorial protesting the seizure of *la Trasmerana*'s cargo on January 1, 1795.[33] But if Moodie was correct, Peronne may well have been present at the incident involving the raid on the warehoused powder described in the memorial of the captains and outfitters:

> Our brave sans culottes ... seized from the magazine the amount of powder they could carry on their backs and loaded it aboard the *Eagle* under the protection of the tricolor. The Americans even took arms to cooperate with our project rather than have the Americans [i.e., their countrymen] turn over to the enemies of our country such a precious cargo under such an iniquitous judgment.[34]

A search of contemporary newspapers, correspondence, and other records has failed to yield any further information on when and where this serious challenge to the authority of the U.S. Government took place or who exactly was involved. It does seem certain, however, that the crew of the privateer *la Carmagnole* was involved, and that the incident probably took place between November 1 and 17, for on November 18 the brig *Eagle,* Latalie, arrived at Charleston from Savannah in company with the privateer schooner *la Carmagnole* and the prize *la Princesa de Asturias*. One is led to conclude that after the raid's proceeds had been loaded in *Eagle,* no time was lost in seeking the more hospitable climate of Charleston.[35]

The action against *la Trasmerana* finally came to trial on January 2, 1795, after having been postponed from its original date of December 4. The indignation, if not the violence, of the privateersmen seems to have been justified, for the Federal District Court of Georgia dismissed Captain Trabudua's libel as

---

American government, have been suffered to be fitted out at Charleston." It was reported that she had taken 20 prizes, most of them Spanish, and that she had 33,000 dollars in specie on board at the time of her capture.

[32] *The City Gazette*, October 27, 1794, mentions that some 50 Frenchmen were set on shore and given their liberty.

[33] "Les Capitaine & Armateurs ... en Rade de Charleston." The signers of the memorial were H. Gariscan, Guillaume Barre, Alexandre Lory, Jean Baptiste Carvin, Bouteille, and others whose names are illegible.

[34] Ibid., translated.

[35] *The City Gazette*, November 18, 1794.

The ship Belisarius *of Salem, 1794, was built with an eye toward privateering as well as trade during the Anglo-American war scare of 1794. Many such vessels found their way into the hands of French privateering entrepreneurs, and Charleston, South Carolina, did a thriving business in their purchase and sale. From a watercolor copy by M. Macpherson of the original by M. Corné. Courtesy the Essex Institute, Salem, Massachusetts.*

unfounded. Whether costs were also assessed against the libelant is not known.[36] Without the records of the case one can only wonder what evidence was adduced to cause the District Court of Georgia to throw out the libel of the Spanish vessel, but one can surmise that the libel's flaw lay in the claim that *Eagle* was fitted out in Charleston, for such certainly was not the case. Perhaps Peronne himself put in an appearance with convincing evidence that he had captured the Spanish ship with *le Républicain*.

Moodie was no more successful with the libel he lodged against *Eagle* than Captain Trabudua had been with his action against *la Trasmerana*. Although he managed to tie the vessel up in litigation until early May 1795, she was finally put up for sale at Beale's Wharf,[37] purchased by Carvin, and given to Peronne as a replacement for the captured *le Républicain*.[38] As *l'Aigle*, she was reported operating, in July 1795 in company with Carvin's *le Vengeur,* in the vicinity of Crooked Island Passage and the north coast of Jamaica. She continued to appear at Charleston until at least January 1796 when both the vessel and her master were defendants in a law suit brought by the chandlery firm of North & Vesey for payments of supplies delivered to the privateer.[39]

---

[36] *Georgia Gazette*, January 8, 1795.

[37] An advertizement for the sale appeared in the *City Gazette*, May 12, 1795.

[38] As early as December 17, 1794, Moodie, writing to his superior in Philadelphia noted that *Eagle* was a remarkably fast sailer and that Peronne meant to have her command (BCC, p. 593).

[39] BEE, *Reports*, pp. 78–79, *North & Vesey* v. *Brig Eagle and Caesar Peronne.*

The fitting out and servicing of French raiders continued to be a major concern of privateer outfitters at Charleston until the summer of 1795, despite Benjamin Moodie's best efforts.

If the Royal Navy had been able to appear off the port at more frequent intervals, as the already quoted Nassau newspaper (see p. 63) hoped would be possible, perhaps the privateering might have been inhibited at an earlier stage. Subsequent to the brief visit of HMS *Hussar* in February 1794, British warships did not make another appearance until mid-August of that year. Thereafter, until the beginning of January 1795, units of Rear Admiral Murray's squadron, including HMS *Quebec,* the frigates *Blonde, Thetis, Terpsichore,* and *Hussar,* and the sloop-of-war *Scorpion* cruised singly or in units of various size in the vicinity of Charleston and Savannah. Their total effect, beyond infuriating Charlestonians by impressing seamen from the American vessels they systematically overhauled entering or leaving harbor, seems to have been negligible.[40]

Hussar and *Scorpion,* whose visit we have already noted in relation to the capture of *le Républicain,* had missed an excellent opportunity to deal privateering a serious blow by failing to capture the Letter of Marque schooner *l'Intrépide* which slipped into Charleston the very day the frigate and sloop-of-war arrived, for Jean Baptiste Carvin had come as a passenger in *l'Intrépide* on one of his regular shuttle trips from Port-de-Paix to oversee the fitting out of two new privateers: the Spanish prize *la Princesa de Asturias,* taken by *le Républicain,* and the brig *le Pichegru* (ex-*Pulaski*). The latter of these was of great concern to Benjamin Moodie who kept a watchful eye on her progress after her purchase by Carvin.

The commander of *le Pichegru* was Henri Garriscan, a former officer of Carvin's who had commanded *l'Industrie* during a September 1794 cruise.[41] As an associate in *le Pichegru* he had taken extreme care in fitting his vessel for sea. When his

---

[40] A Letter of Marque from Guadeloupe, the schooner *la Liberté*, was delayed from leaving port between August 22 and September 14, 1795, when she made a dash for sea (see, *City Gazette* for that period of time) and the privateer *la Montagne* was brought to bay off Edisto while two of her prizes were chased ashore (*City Gazette*, April 18, 19, 23, 1794.)

[41] Garriscan held a provisional grade of Lieutenant de Vaisseau in the French Navy, issued by General Laveaux. He was to become a successful privateer commander and his *le Pandour* became known to American seamen in the Caribbean during the Quasi-War with France.

request for clearance was denied on the grounds that it contravened United States neutrality laws, and three separate searches yielded nothing to substantiate the charge, Garriscan became righteously indignant.[42] After he had fumed to Fonspertuis about his perishable cargo, the consul finally managed to have the ship cleared out for Port-de-Paix. But Moodie, who was responsible for lodging the information, was again able to delay the sailing of the vessel until HM frigate *Thetis* once more showed up off the bar. It was not until the end of the first week of January 1795 that *le Pichegru* managed to slip out to sea.

Between January 1795, when *le Pichegru* sailed, and the beginning of July 1795, the outfitting of French privateers reached its peak of activity. It was a particular time of trial for consul Moodie as well. Added to the frustrations he was suffering in the U.S. District Court, and the dark suspicions that he harbored about the good will of State and Federal officials in carrying out the impartial enforcement of United States neutrality laws, was the worry about the seamen from captured British merchant ships turned loose on the town. It was important to keep these men at hand as witnesses for cases in litigation, and this drew heavily on the slim contingency fund Moodie used to fight the French raiders in the law courts. If these seamen were not subsidized they would readily sign on with the French raiders, lured by the prospects of prize money or merely to keep from starvation in the streets, since no international convention protected them.[43] On the other hand, the predilection of seamen of whatever nation to go privateering under whatever flag, was used by Moodie to good effect, for it enabled him to plant spies among the privateersmen and obtain intelligence of plans being hatched and learn what vessels were fitting out as raiders.[44]

Early in March 1795 Moodie was confronted by a particularly vexing situation. A very valuable Jamaican merchantman

---

[42] "Copie de la Pétition addressée au Citoyen Conssul [sic] par Gariscan, capitaine du navire Le pichegru," dated "Charleston le 11 nivose L'an 3eme [December 31, 1794]."

[43] Public Records Office, London, 133 Foreign Office 55/11, Moodie to Murray, Charleston, April 25, 1795. Moodie refers to the inadequacy of the subsistence guaranteed to seamen of the Royal Navy—9 pence per diem as not being "sufficient to buy firewood in this expensive place."

[44] Ibid., Foreign Office 97/98, March 12, 1795. This letter contains material on the French privateer cited below.

4: PALATINATE CHALLENGES NEUTRALITY

had put into Charleston for emergency repair and was ready to proceed on her voyage. How was he to get her safely to sea, with the approaches to the port infested by prowling raiders and with five other raiders lying in the harbor apparently ready for sea at a moment's notice?

Two of those in the harbor were notably successful privateers: Alexander Bolchos' *la Parisienne*, "remarkably fast and manned by Desperadoes of all Nations," and *la Mère Michel*, a medium-sized schooner of 50 tons but carrying a very heavy armament of 12 to 15 guns.[45] The three other raiders, newly arrived, included *le Courier National*, mounting 16 guns, copper bottomed, and "a fast sailer though an old vessel," [46] and "a 14-gun Bermuda-built ship which had formerly been a Spanish Packet," painted black with a head and galleries. Moodie was impressed by the detail that her iron guns "were painted green to represent brass." This vessel, of course, was Carvin's prize *la Princesa de Asturias*.[47] The third vessel was the old frigate *le Dauphin* (ex-*Delaware*), mounting between 24 and 32 guns; Bouteille had managed to work his way out of his troubles with the port authorities (see p. 75) and had completed the repairs to her, which earlier had been halted. Moodie commented particularly on her "very much altered appearance." The upper deck had been entirely razed, her old ports had been opened and her old head and quarter galleries removed. She was painted a funereal black. Moodie then observed without further comment that the work had been done "with a view of making her look like a Collier or a North Country built ship." [48]

---

[45] Ibid. Considering her size, the reported armament is improbable. *La Mère Michel* was a relative newcomer. It is not certain that she was fitted out at Charleston but she was certainly owned there. She arrived at Charleston March 1, 1795, after having sent in the British ship *Eliza* of Jamaica (*City Gazette*, February 10, 1795) and, in partnership with *le Général Laveaux*, *la Tendre Mère* (ibid., February 16, 1795). An Edenton, North Carolina, newspaper reported the raider's arrival at that port on February 2 and that she had taken 2 ships, 2 brigs, 2 schooners, and 1 sloop (ibid., February 16, 1795).

[46] BCC, p. 593. Moodie refers to her simply as the "Courier of Liverpool." This vessel had been taken prize by the privateer *le Port-de-Paix* and her tender *le Petit Port-de-Paix* in October 1794 and brought into Charleston on October 24. Within one week she was condemned, and hull and cargo were put up for sale. (*The City Gazette*, October 24 and 30, 1794) Moodie libelled the prize and succeeded in delaying the captors until January 1795, when his suit was dismissed with costs (BCC, p. 590).

[47] See above, p. 79.

[48] Such disguises were not uncommon. In this instance it is conceivable that it

Moodie may well have asked himself, did these vessels make up another Saint Domingue shuttle fleet, such as those which had been dispatched with provisions and powder earlier, or did the unusual features presented by these vessels portend another use? These questions, when compounded with rumors of the imminent arrival from Port-de-Paix of the former British frigate *Hyaena*,[49] which had been refitted under the tricolor at Port-de-Paix, must have made the situation seem most threatening.

On March 12, Moodie addressed a dispatch to Rear Admiral Murray in HMS *Cleopatra,* thought to be cruising in the vicinity, or to the first of His Majesty's ships that could be found, and sent it to sea in a chartered pilot boat under a Mr. Giles. The dispatch requested that a British man-of-war be sent to escort the Jamaican merchantman across the Gulf Stream. He also apprised the admiral of the situation in Charleston, saying that his spies had informed him that the French privateersmen were threatening to kill British prisoners. Admiral Murray would be well advised, wrote Moodie, to question prisoners from French privateers closely on this matter.

There is evidence that a British warship did come to Moodie's aid and that the Jamaican got off safely to sea. As for the raiders, if a joint operation had been planned there is no evidence that it was carried out.[50] But for Moodie the respite was brief; on April 8 *le Pichegru*, now named *le Brutus Français*, was once again in Charleston armed with 16 6-pounders and 2 car-

---

was planned to slip *Delaware* into a British convoy under the cover of night to await a favorable opportunity to make a strike. Privateersmen often resorted to disguise to throw off inquisitive enemy men-of-war while sailing under a neutral flag. Rigs were often altered at sea, and Garriscan's *le Pandour* appeared as a blacksided schooner from one side and a yellowsided schooner from the other.

[49] On March 19, 1795 the *City Gazette* published a letter from Port-de-Paix to Fonspertuis which told of the French victories in the Caribbean and stated that the corvette *Hyaena* would be ready to sail for the continent within 20 days.

[50] *Le Dauphin* (ex-*Delaware*) seems finally to have put to sea, bound for Port-de-Paix. *La Mère Michel* cleared out toward the end of March on a 30-day cruise (*Georgia Gazette*, May 7, 1795) and returned with the British 6-gun ship *Phoebe* and the brig *Tivoli* as prizes. A subsequent cruise ended in her capture in late June by a New Providence privateer of 20 guns (*Georgia Gazette*, July 16, 1795).

La Parisienne continued her successful raiding career, accounting for at least 14 prizes between the time she sailed in mid-March and December 1795, when it was her misfortune to run ashore and break up on Watling Key. (*City Gazette*, January 4, 1796).

Le Courier Nationale apparently cleared Charleston toward the end of March and made for Guadeloupe to take part in Victor Hugues' campaign against the

ronades, bearing a Saint Domingue commission and still under the command of Garriscan.[51]

Le Brutus had proved her worth during a 30-day cruise by capturing 9 prizes. Nearing Charleston on April 6, Garriscan met with and engaged the Bermudian privateer-ship *Sir Charles Grey*, Daniel Morgan, armed with 16 12-pounders. This vessel had been lurking about the approaches, intercepting French prizes bound in for that port. One of these was Garriscan's prize, *Alfred*, which had been run ashore while attempting to cross the bar. If the engagement had been inconclusive, at least the Bermudian was sufficiently damaged to force her to draw off and abandon further harassment of the French raiders.[52]

Le Brutus' return to Charleston was in reality a waystop dictated perhaps by the need to consult with the vessel's agent about the disposition of prizes and to transact business with Carvin, whose latest privateer, *la Princesa de Asturias*, was being readied for sea. On April 21 the two vessels sailed in company and within two days after their departure they ran into a force of four British warships, two ships-of-the-line and two frigates, perhaps the very vessels which Moodie had sent Giles' pilot boat to pursue, more than a month before. The two Frenchmen parted company, each chased by a frigate and a 74. After three days and three nights, *le Brutus* gave her pursuers the slip after heaving over the side four guns and taking to her sweeps.

When Garriscan arrived at Philadelphia he wrote back to Charleston of the incident and expressed the opinion that Carvin must certainly have outrun his pursuers, since *la Princesa*

British islands. On July 3, 1795, the *City Gazette* carried the news of her capture off Guadeloupe by a British frigate after an obstinate engagement.

[51] From what can be gleaned of her activities in the vicinity of Philadelphia in May and still later in New York, *le Brutus* seemed to be acting more in the capacity of a naval auxilary than a privateer. Her movements between the United States and the West Indies indicate that she might have been used in carrying dispatches.

[52] Two of *le Brutus'* prizes—the Spanish schooner *Santo Christo de la Caridad*, Montechristi for Havana, and the polacre *Nuestra Senora del Carmen*, Barcelona for Havana—were reported as entering Savannah (*Georgia Gazette*, April 9); two others, Spanish slavers, were reported as having been ransomed for 41,000 dollars. *Alfred* was refloated on the next tide and taken up to Charleston, where Moodie libelled her on the grounds that *le Brutus* had been fitted out at Charleston. Bee found for the respondents. When Moodie brought the case to the Circuit Court, the judgment of the lower court was confirmed, and then carried it to the Supreme Court, where once again the decree of the lower court was confirmed. (See *Moodie v. the Ship Alfred*, 3 Dallas 307 (1796).)

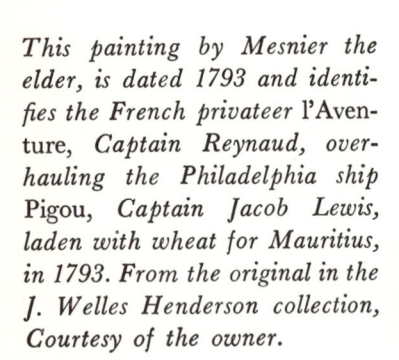

This painting by Mesnier the elder, is dated 1793 and identifies the French privateer l'Aventure, Captain Reynaud, overhauling the Philadelphia ship Pigou, Captain Jacob Lewis, laden with wheat for Mauritius, in 1793. From the original in the J. Welles Henderson collection, Courtesy of the owner.

handily outsailed his vessel.[53] *Le Brutus* sailed south from Philadelphia for the West Indies where Garriscan became involved in Victor Hugues' effort to carry the war to the British. Except for a single call in January 1796, *le Brutus* never put in at Charleston again.

As for *la Princesa*, Garriscan was right about her escape. She reached Port-de-Paix and quickly emerged as *le Vengeur de Sans Culottes*, or, more simply, *le Vengeur*.[54] She was reported as operating in the vicinity of Crooked Island passage on May 21, 1795, in company with another of Carvin's privateers, *la Carmagnole*, a schooner of 8 guns, commanded by Captain Lory,[55] and shortly thereafter the two vessels were reported

---

[53] *City Gazette*, March 30, 1795. Extract of a letter from Garriscan in Philadelphia. While at Philadelphia, the crew of *le Brutus* on May 30 became involved in a fray with some workmen at a ropewalk. Garriscan took the occasion of a city magistrate's dealing with the rioters to deliver some unflattering observations on American hospitality. These were printed in the *City Gazette*, June 22, 1795 (datelined Philadelphia, May 30).

[54] Two other *Vengeurs* seem to share the scene, one being referred to as *le Vengeur de Risque-tout*, the other simply as *le Vengeur*, both of which called at Charleston and Savannah. Of these, the first seems to be identifiable with Carvin's vessel. The second appeared after June 1795, the month in which, it has been established, Carvin's vessel was set afire in the Bahamas.

[55] *La Carmagnole* made her appearance at Charleston first on November 18, after having participated in the affair of *la Trasmerana*'s cargo (see above, p. 79). She was one of Carvin's most successful investments and made use of the port of Charleston well into 1796.

cruising off the north coast of Jamaica between Port Maria and Orracabella in plain sight of shore. According to a letter recounting the capture of the British ship *Hero* by the two privateers, "they both intended to follow the [Jamaica] convoy through the gulf, as they tell me, which I have not the least doubt of, for they seem to be perfectly acquainted with the situation of the island." [56]

The magnet that drew the French privateers away from Charleston by the summer of 1795 was, of course, the opening up, in the very heart of the Caribbean, of new privateering opportunities brought about not only by the revival of offensive

Detail of this handsome painting, which is possibly unique for the period 1793–1802 in its representation of a sharp-built privateer schooner of uncontestably American design operating under the French flag.

---

[56] *Georgia Gazette*, August 6, 1795: "Extract of a letter from aboard HMS Sloop of War *le Serin* [sic], Mole St. Nicholas, May 30, [1795]." *Hero* never did reach Charleston, for she was run ashore on the Isle of Pines through an error of navigation by her prizemaster (*Georgia Gazette*, July 30, 1795). Two other prizes taken

strength in Saint Domingue under Laveaux and André Rigaud, who was in command of the Department of the South, but, more fundamentally, by Victor Hugues' expanding operations in the Lesser Antilles. These, as we have noted (p. 64), had temporarily paralyzed Britain's war effort throughout the Caribbean.

Even before the final evacuation of Guadeloupe by the British in December 1794, Victor Hugues had gone on the offensive. A small reinforcement from France temporarily allowed him to send out combined flotillas of warships and privateers to harry the approaches to the Caribbean from the latitude of Barbados to Puerto Rico. Britain's hard-worked Caribbean squadrons were accordingly thrown off balance, and her forces were held to the defensive well into 1796 by interminable delays caused by mismanagement and a series of disasters involving reinforcements from England.

On March 2, 1795, after a carefully prepared campaign of subversion had been launched throughout the British islands of the Caribbean and in Spanish Trinidad, Hugues' storm—which the British called the Brigand's War—broke over the West Indies. A series of insurrections flared on island after island, leaving confusion and terror in their wake. Grenada, lying close to the chief British staging area at Barbados, was the first target. There, as at other islands, local insurrectionaries were joined by French expeditionary forces carried by privateers from Guadeloupe. Three days after the outbreak at Grenada, St. Vincent flared up in revolt. The Caribs, long discontented with British rule and carefully propagandized by Hugues' agents were reinforced by French troops and arms and ammunition ferried over to them under the cover of night by privateers.

St. Lucia was taken under attack on April 1 and the entire island passed into French hands when the last of the British garrison was evacuated on June 19.

To increase the confusion among the British and their French royalist allies, Hugues bombarded the entire Antilles with

---

from the convoy, however, did reach Charleston about July 12, the brigs *Kingston* and *Potowmac* (*Georgia Gazette*, July 16, 1795). These were preceded by the arrival of *le Vengeur* and *la Carmagnole* at Savannah (*Georgia Gazette*, July 2, 1795). *Potowmac* was subsequently libeled, and as late as March 23, 1796, Phineas Bond, British chargé d'affaires at Philadelphia, wrote that the Supreme Court had continued the *Potowmac* case and that the counsel was not sanguine about the outcome (BCC, Annex 7, p. 621). For reasons unknown, *Kingston*'s capture was not disputed in court.

4: PALATINATE CHALLENGES NEUTRALITY

promises of emancipation to the slave populations and bloodcurdling proclamations threatening reprisals for any Republicans who were executed and the guillotine to any Frenchman who joined the British.

As Hugues struck to windward at Grenada, St. Lucia, and St. Vincents and threatened landings on Martinique itself—the nerve center of the British war effort in the Lesser Antilles—the Royal Navy drew off units from the Leeward Islands. Hugues struck unerringly in that direction.

The neutral Danish islands of St. Croix and St. Thomas, which under a combination of Hugues' merciless browbeating and a hunger for profits had become a major source of supply for Guadeloupe and a haven for French privateers, became an unwilling host to an expeditionary force aimed at Dutch St. Eustatius.

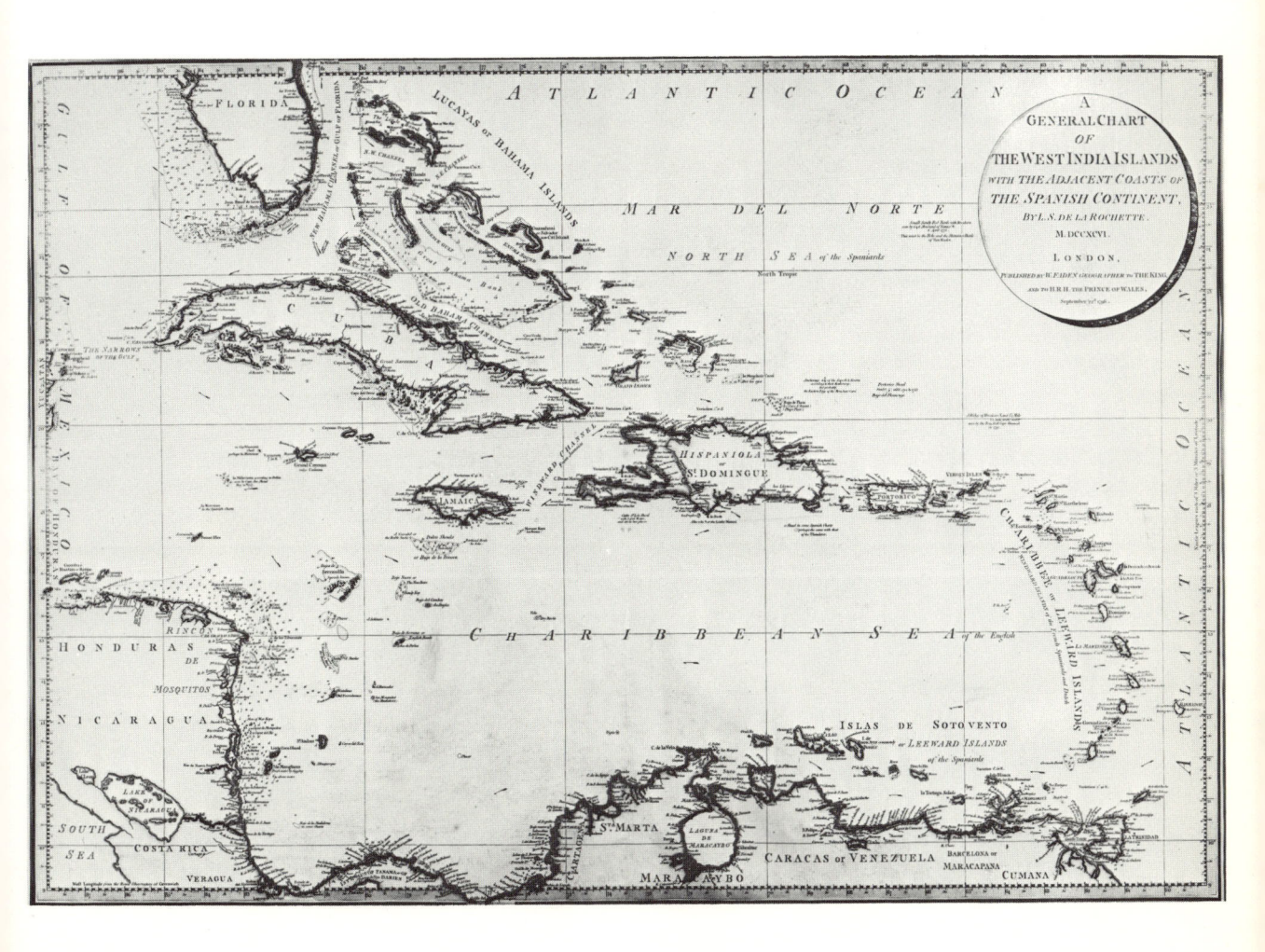

At St. Kitts, John Stanley, President of the island's Assembly, fearful of the consequences of French possession of the Dutch island, urgently called for aid from Martinique, only to receive the despairing answer that St. Eustatius must be left to its fate.

By mid-April not only St. Eustatius but St. Martins were in French hands, while belatedly dispatched British naval units sailed about in bewilderment attempting to fend off the threat to neighboring British islands.

By June 23, 1795, the situation of the British in the West Indies was such that the Barbados *Mercury* lamented:

> Thus stands affairs:
> Guadeloupe long since taken.
> Martinico Attempted.
> St. Lucia Abandoned.
> Grenada ruined.
> St. Vincents laid waste.
> Antigua unsafe and
> Dominico on the verge of being lost.

In the midst of this calamitous situation to which the West Indies are now reduced, Barbados still remains secure. How long this may be, the virtue of her sons can only determine.

Chapter 5

JAY'S TREATY: THE "GREAT BETRAYAL"

THE HIGH TIDE OF FRENCH PRIVATEERING out of the port of Charleston that had been reached between January and July 1795, began to ebb rapidly, but during that brief period, Charleston wore an air that caused a London newspaper to characterize it as "a province of France" and "a disgrace to the thirteen United States."[1]

Public celebrations sponsored by the democratic and patriotic societies flourished as they had in previous years,[2] but none of these outdid the public demonstration of grief of the Society of the Sans Culottes at the news of the death of General Dugommier, whose victories in the Pyrenees brought Spain to sue for peace. A *décadi's* mourning was decreed and, said an announcement, "the Republic [sic] thunder on board the armed vessels in the road shall salute on the morning and evening of the first day [of mourning]; that on all days of said decade, ensigns of distress shall be displayed on board of the vessels—that each day a discharge of cannon shall recall to the

---

[1] *City Gazette*, June 8, 1795, datelined London, March 25 [1795].
[2] On January 21, 1795, all good "sans culottes" assembled on Bequet's Green to renew their civic oaths and to sing patriotic hymns. A parade through town followed, accompanied by a band of music and the martial sound of cannons fired from French shipping in the harbor. The same evening, Citizen Michel, the owner of the successful privateer *la Mère Michel* tendered an elegant ball to celebrate the occasion. (*City Gazette*, January 21, 1795.)

Republicans in mourning the great loss they have sustained." [3]

As has been noted (p. 37), during 1794 rioting had taken on a more vicious character and public reaction to it had become sharper. By April 1795, the City Council was obliged to deal with a particularly ugly outbreak of hooliganism which resulted in a death by stabbing.[4] But the city Intendent pro tem, John Edwards, had to deal with an even more serious challenge to peace and order when a "large party of Frenchmen armed with swords and daggers . . . forcibly rescued . . . Anthony Shepland, alias Cadet, Jean Michael and John Cutteau while under committment for riot and assault" from constables who had them in security. A sizable reward was offered for the apprehending and delivery of the three men to the gaoler of Charleston.[5] The outraged citizenry demanded that the Intendent take counsel with the Governor "respecting the most proper measures to be adopted for the tranquility of the city." Some expressed the opinion that nothing short of prohibiting armed vessels from approaching the town closer than Fort Johnson would solve the problem. Shore leave for privateer crews, except for officers, was to be rigidly restricted and, when permitted, only under the command of an officer who would be accountable for the peaceful behavior of the men. None were to be armed.[6]

Another aspect of lawlessness indulged in by the privateers' commanders was regarded with even more alarm than infrac-

---

[3] *City Gazette*, May 5, 1795, "Translated from *le Patriote Français*, a French paper just published in this City."

[4] *City Gazette*, February 19, 1795, "Proclamation, the peace and tranquility of the city is much disturbed . . . several persons while walking the streets were wounded at several times . . . 30 dollars reward for information and conviction . . . ."

[5] *City Gazette*, April 23, 1795. The incident took place on April 22. Shepland, or Antoine Chaplin, to give him his proper name, was mate of the French privateer *la Guillotine* then in port. Chaplin made good his escape and soon after was reported molesting American shipping off Port-de-Paix. General Laveaux alarmed by manifestations of outlawry and violence, which began to appear by the fall of 1795, was determined to make an example of Chaplin and paraded him in chains in the streets and forced him to pay a heavy fine. (For details see *City Gazette*, November 10, 1795, datelined New York, November 3, "Extracts of a letter from Port-de-Paix, October 11, 1795.")

[6] *City Gazette*, April 24, 1795, reporting the minutes of the City Council on the previous day. At the same meeting an ordinance was read for the first time forbidding mariners from appearing in the streets of Charleston "with swords, pistols or any other offensive weapons under the penalty not to exceed £20 for each offense," offenders were to be proceeded against in the court of the wardens, with the fine to go to the informers.

tions against the peace and order of the city. This stemmed from their activities in the forbidden slave trade.[7] Charlestonians had shown great forbearance in allowing the entry of slaves belonging to refugees from Saint Domingue in spite of apprehensions held of the possible evil effect they might have on domestic slaves. To counteract possible subversion, a system of surveillance was set up to detect and stop the transfer of the infection of egalitarian notions brought in not only by the Saint Domingue slaves but by the outpouring of philanthropic propaganda from the French dominated "clubs." [8]

In April 1794 a wave of consternation had been caused by the appearance of a Spanish prize belonging to the French privateer *la Montagne* carrying a partial cargo of slaves, especially since Santo Domingan slaves were reputed to be of "bad character." [9] An anxious committee of citizens inquired into what certainly must have been a collusive infraction of the slave importation act. Each of the 75 slaves was carefully accounted for; 12 had died, 7 who were serving as sailors had made good their escape, 6 had been sent by water to Augusta, Georgia, and 50 remained on hand. The committee was finally mollified by the commander of the privateer who pledged that he would carry the remainder out of the State and use diligence in recovering the runaways. To this the privateer agent Abraham Sasportas promised his assistance.

The pernicious effect of the presence of the French-owned slaves was debated hotly for the rest of 1794. In June, at a

---

[7] The slave trade had been prohibited in South Carolina in 1787. As a result of the slave upheavals in Saint Domingue in 1793, the prohibition had been reenacted. It must be noted that in the neighboring state of Georgia the slave trade flourished.

[8] Colonel A. Vanderhorst of the Charleston Militia on August 26, 1793, issued an order which he had received "this moment" from Governor Moultrie that patrol duty was to be regularly performed and that negro houses "or any other suspected places" were to be searched. If arms were found they were to be sent to Charleston. Large meetings of negroes were to be suppressed and militiamen were to be careful to look out for any tendency of negroes to revolt. (Order Book, 30th Regiment 7th Brigade, South Carolina Militia, 1793–1814.)

The depth of apprehension that some held on this subject may be gauged by an extract from a letter published by the *New York Journal and Patriotic Register* on October 11, 1793: "They write from Charleston, S.C. the NEGROES have become so insolent in so much that the citizens are alarmed and keep a constant guard. It is said that St. Domingue negroes have sown the seed of revolt and that a magazine has been attempted to be broken open."

[9] *South Carolina State Gazette*, April 10, 1794.

public meeting, a Mr. Hunt offered the proposition that "all negroes without exception that have within the last three years arrived here from the French West Indies be expelled."[10] Under the pen name "Rusticus" a Charlestonian went Mr. Hunt one better by demanding that all French refugees as well as their slaves be deported, asserting that the safety and prosperity of the country was at stake.

In July Rusticus, who apparently never succeeded in breaking into print, again sought to express his concern over the slave situation. Prompted by reports which appeared in the *Columbian Herald* of July 14, 1794, which chronicled Laveaux's triumph on Saint Domingue and which attributed much of his success to the effect of the French slave emancipation decree on his negro troops, *Rusticus* declared himself scandalized that a Charleston newspaper should publish such a report:

> I never expected that in a paper published by one of our own citizens that the tribute of praise should be so lavishly bestowed upon a race of men who by their example and success hold up every inducement to our domestics to resist our authority and rise up in arms against us.... They are told that actuated by the spirit of liberty their Brethren have become heroes ... I will not dwell upon the consequences. Your good sense will point out the propriety of preventing a repetition of similar publications.

On August 7, *Rusticus* sounded the tocsin in yet another letter. "It has been asserted that there actually exists within our city a Society corresponding with that which the French term *Les Amis des Noirs.*"

On September 5, however, still another incident of slave importation brought forth a public meeting at the Charleston Exchange. A committee of "distinguished citizens" was appointed to examine the details of the importation of 22 Negroes from Santo Domingo in the brig *Governor Pinckney,* Captain Conolly.[11] The committee's report was published in *The City Gazette* on September 8, 1794. Both Captain Conolly and the ubiquitous Jean François Théric had produced the 22 slaves, 17 of whom were lodged in the workhouse for safekeeping. The remaining 5, consisting of 2 free women and their children,

---

[10] Quoted in MS. letter "Rusticus" to "Gentlemen," dated June 20, 1794. (File 235, Charleston Historical Society, Charleston, South Carolina.) Rusticus is believed to be Alexander Garden, Jr., author of *Anecdotes of the Revolution.*

[11] *City Gazette*, September 9, 1794. The committee consisted of Thomas Simmons, chairman, Theodore Gaillard, Jr., Benjamin Huger, J. Rutledge, and Solomon Legare, Jr.

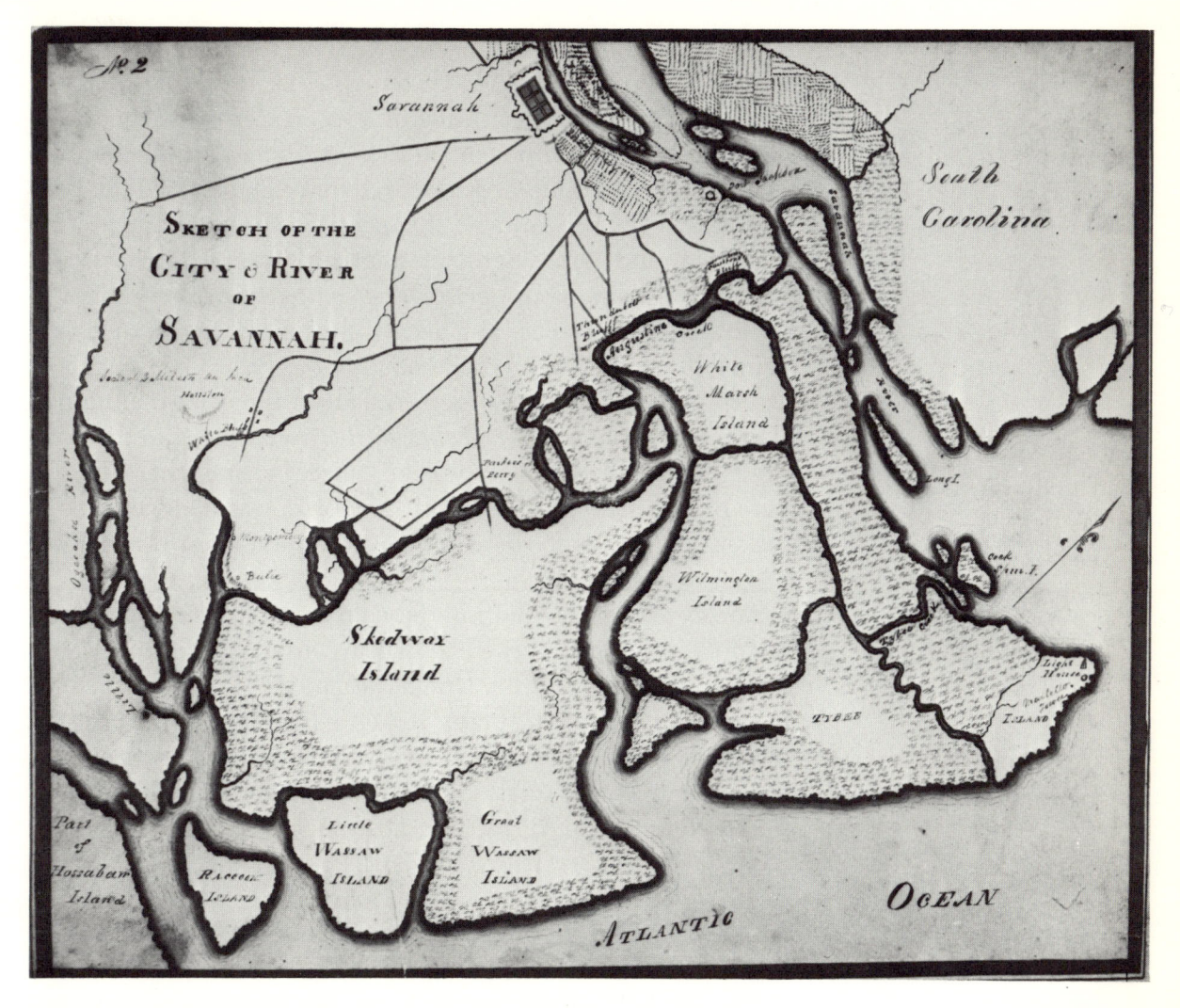

"Sketch of the City & River of Savannah," about 1815. Original in the United States National Archives, record group 77, no. 37.

were kept on board the *Governor Pinckney*. When the brig was ready to sail, the workhouse would deliver the slaves, and the Committee would make a final accounting at that time.[12]

But neither the lawlessness of the privateersmen nor their role in the illegal introduction of slaves into the State of South Carolina, nor yet concern with potential slave insurrection had the least effect toward diminishing the activities of the French raiders. As far as the legal aspect of French privateering was concerned, the United States District and Circuit Courts of South Carolina seemed bent on favoring the raiders.

Such was not the case, however, in the neighboring State of Georgia. At Savannah the riotous living of the privateersmen, their disregard of the law, and the chicanery of their

---

[12] From the lack of further news on the matter of the 22 slaves it can be concluded that *Pinckney* sailed without further incident and with her cargo on board.

agents had, by early 1794, become a stink in the noses of the sober burghers. The recruiting of a foreign army on the soil of Georgia and the impudent attack on the warehouse storing *la Trasmerana*'s gunpowder seems to have determined the Federal Courts to discourage the privateersmen from entering Savannah and disposing of their prizes there, as the proceedings in the cases of the prizes *Everton* and *Elizabeth* serve to illustrate. The former had been captured by the French privateer *l'Egalité* (ex-*l'Ami de la Pointe-à-Pitre*) at the end of December 1794. The libel served against the prize maintained that since *l'Egalité* and *la Pointe-à-Pitre* were one and the same vessel, and that the latter was an "illegal armament," the seizure of the *Everton* was illegal. The prize was handed back to her owners although there was never a question of the validity of *l'Egalite*'s commission.

Elizabeth was carried into Savannah as a prize to *l'Ami de la Pointe-à-Pitre* in May 1794. British consul Moodie, motivated by the decision on the Dutch brigantine *Vrouw Christina Magdalena,* urged Captain Ross to libel his former vessel, which he did in November. On December 19, a decision was rendered in favor of the libelant and upheld in the United States Circuit Court for the District of South Carolina in May 1795.[13]

Among the friends of the French privateersmen at Savannah, indignation aroused by the *Elizabeth* decision was voiced in an extract of a letter published in the Charleston *City Gazette* of July 18, 1795. Referring to Judge Blair's decision the writer mentioned that—

> He also gave a decree of over seventy-five thousand dollars against Hill, Mag and Woodbridge of this city. It appeared that they were agents for the privateer which sent into this port a ship called Elizabeth: they sold the ship and cargo as such and paid over to the French consul the amount of the sales of the ship and cargo. This decree passed notwithstanding it was proved that the ship and cargo were advertised and sold by a publicly licensed auctioneer and the sale was not forbid. How far those decrees will be justified with you I cannot say, but I hope your judges of the United States [Courts] will never confirm so iniquitous a decree.[14]

Certainly French privateering interests at Charleston could not have levelled such charges against the Federal courts in South Carolina, where the United States Circuit Court of Appeals, arrived at Charleston on October 24, 1794, in the

---

[13] *Talbot* v. *Janson*, 3 Dallas 133 (1795).
[14] The letter was datelined Savannah, May 10, 1795.

person of Associate Justice James Wilson and opened its sessions the next day with Judge Bee in attendance.[15] Between sittings at Charleston and Columbia the court dealt with a heavy load of admiralty cases, some pending for over a year.[16] During this time it reviewed decisions made by the District Court on 14 appeals of cases in admiralty. Of these, Benjamin Moodie alone had lodged 9 in behalf of British owners. The 12 cases in which the lower court decision was in favor of the French privateersmen were confirmed. And the 2 cases in which the District Court had held against the privateersmen, were reversed by the Circuit Court.[17]

Yet as high as resentment ran in mid-1795 against the more nefarious activities of the French privateersmen, it was eclipsed by the nationwide furor caused by the revelation of the terms of the Jay Treaty. As early as March, Charleston had already become aware of the contents of the treaty, which had been signed on November 19, 1794, and, as elsewhere in the United States, the debate over its provisions and implications for the future was pre-empting wide attention.

The French benefited by the outrage vented on what was held to be an abject surrender to British arrogance. Charleston's American Independence Day celebrations were attended by the French societies and old ties were recalled, and on Bastille Day Charlestonians took advantage of the occasion to declare

---

[15] *The City Gazette*, October 27, 1794.
[16] The court finally adjourned on November 5, 1795.
[17] The cases decided were the following (*City Gazette*, November 6, 1795):

Appellant	Respondent	Decision of District Judge
Lavergne and others	J. Arnold	Affirmed
Benjamin Moodie, vice consul of his Britannic Majesty	Ship *Mermaid*	Affirmed
"	Brig *Eliza*	Affirmed
"	Ship *Phyn*	Affirmed
"	Brig *Tivoli*	Affirmed
"	Brig *Favorite*	Affirmed
"	Ship *Brothers*	Affirmed
Lawrence Vidal	Benjamin Moodie	Reversed
John Mitchel	John Geyer	Reversed
Benjamin Moodie	Ship *Alfred*	Affirmed
"	Ship *Britannia*	Affirmed
"	Ship *Phoebe Ann*	Affirmed
"	Snow *Potowmack*	Affirmed
Don Diogo Morphy (sic) Consul of his Catholic Majesty	Ship *Sacra Familia*	Affirmed

their admiration for the principles of the French Revolution and to pledge Franco-American solidarity. The interval between the two holidays was marked by the appearance of the full text of Jay's Treaty. A *City Gazette Extraordinary* was published on Sunday, July 12,[18] and it was at once clear that should the treaty's article 24 be put into effect, the doom of French privateering out of American ports would be certain and final. The article stipulated that the United States would undertake not only to prevent the arming of privateers of Britain's enemies but to deny the French permission to sell their prizes as they had hitherto done, or even to purchase provisions beyond those necessary to take them to the nearest French port.

To the Francophile, the Treaty represented a staggering United States betrayal of an old friend; to those mainly concerned with the future of American trade as well as national honor, it portended an incalculable financial blow. Bitterness was great on the day after publication of its text. American ships in the harbor of Charleston lowered their colors to half mast and kept them there until sunset to express their "disapprobation of the Treaty."[19] On July 16 a heated public meeting, presided over by Chief Justice of the Supreme Court of the United States John Rutledge, was held to decide how best to make known their feeling about the "reprehensible" Treaty.[20] A select committee was elected and instructed to draw up a report. Published on July 24, the report urged the suspension of article 12,[21] except for the clause protecting American seamen from impressment. Articles 23, 24, and 25 were also rejected

---

[18] The editorial comment preceding the text of the treaty is of interest: "As it is possible that the news of the Treaty, between the United States and Great Britain, being in town, might agitate the minds of the citizens so strongly, that they would not be able to give a due attention to the religious duties of the day, until they first should have seen it. The Publisher of the City Gazette, therefore, thought proper to issue a Gazette Extraordinary on the occasion, which they hope will not be deemed an intrusion on the sanctity of the Sabbath.

"The Treaty was received here yesterday afternoon, by the ship Alexander, Captain Gault, seven days from Philadelphia."

[19] *City Gazette*, July 14, 1795.

[20] *City Gazette*, July 17, 1795: "Before the question was put, the Intendent in a very forcible manner, recommended to the citizens to be calm and temperate in the discussion of this momentous affair, and to discountenance any appearance of disorder or riot."

[21] This restricted American trade to the West Indies to vessels of 70 tons or under and specified under what conditions the trade could be carried on.

5 : JAY'S TREATY—THE GREAT BETRAYAL

as having a tendency "to make our seaport towns scenes of riot and bloodshed." These articles, the report went on, also "tend to make a common cause between the United States and Great Britain, to oppress and distress our allies." The report concluded that if the treaty was ratified, the committee apprehended great evils and urged an address to the President that it not be ratified.[22]

The same meeting that heard the report of the select committee heard Charles Pinckney accuse Jay of bartering away the Nation's honor for a mess of pottage. He characterized the treaty as a "mean ungenerous desertion of the interests of our friends the French to whose supplies, at least in the articles they consider as of necessity in their present noble and unexampled struggle for freedom, we were bound by every tie of gratitude and honor to attend to." John Jay, Pinckney stated, should be impeached.[23]

It is not surprising that as the realities of the Jay Treaty began to be appreciated in Charleston's privateering circles, the attractiveness of Amelia Island's port of Saint Marys as a haven for French raiders increased. Privateering interests had expanded greatly in numbers, influence, and wealth over the year before, when Mangourit had barely been able to scrape up four or five raiders to cover the projected East Florida Expedition. By mid-June 1795, the privateersmen and the popular societies had already began to assemble supplies and money. Consul Fonspertuis was deep in negotiations with the remnants of the East Florida expedition, who had taken refuge on the United States side of the Saint Marys River. There a French consular agent had been established and was fanning the smouldering discontent of the Anglo-Spanish settlers between the Saint John and Saint Marys River; he let it be known everywhere that France was willing to underwrite an uprising with powerful aid.[24]

In the latter half of June, an uprising in East Florida broke out under Elijah Rogers, John McIntosh, and Richard Lang, all of whom had participated in the expedition.

---

[22] *City Gazette*, July 23, 1795.
[23] *City Gazette*, August 4, 1795.
[24] Excellent analyses and accounts of the troubles along the river border between Spanish East Florida and the State of Georgia are contained in the East Florida Papers, Library of Congress, Manuscript Division, vol. 26 [M2], box 103 [L8]. See especially, letters from Governor of Florida (Nepomucena de Quesada) and the Captain General of Cuba [Florida and Louisiana] (Las Casas) June 28, 1795.

Lang, who had escaped from a Spanish jail, led a band of insurgents along the Saint John River, where he seized two fortified posts and a Spanish gunboat. With the latter he raided along the River, destroying crops and driving off cattle. By June 28 the rebels dominated the heights along the Camino Real that joined the Saint John and Saint Marys Rivers. Lang, boasting that he had received considerable supplies and the strongest assurances of support from the French, announced that he was ready to march against Saint Augustine itself.[25]

From his vantage point in Charleston, Diogo Morphy (sic), the Spanish consular agent, did his best to keep Saint Augustine alerted to French plans. He warned the Governor of East Florida, Nepomucena de Quesada, on July 22 that the main target of the French filibusterers was Amelia Island. The French interest, wrote Morphy, "was to hold a port where prizes could be carried and disposed of without opposition." As for the Americans interested in the rebellion, Morphy explained, they were eager to procure the benefits of free trade that would result between the United States and a French-controlled Florida.[26]

But even as Morphy wrote, the insurgents struck at Amelia Island under the leadership of J. B. E. Ferrey, who was said to be a French naval lieutenant. The Spanish garrison, taken by surprise, fled without firing a shot and the French flag rose over what was hoped would become a French entrepôt and privateer haven removed from all possibility of interference by an unfriendly United States.

When Joseph Fauchet, then engaged in a losing battle at Philadelphia to influence Congress to reject the Jay Treaty, became aware of Fonspertuis' maneuvering is not clear. Fonspertuis' enemies, as had those of Mangourit, besieged the French Embassy with charges against him that could not be ignored, but before Fauchet was able to find a suitable replace-

---

[25] *City Gazette*, July 9, 1795. "Extracts of a letter from St. Mary's to his friend at Savannah, dated June 30."

A gloomy letter from St. Augustine, dated June 29 published in the *City Gazette*, July 11, 1795, seemed to confirm this state of affairs: "We are badly situated here; but for the fear the letter may be stopped and perused, I dare not tell you the various alarms some are under." The recipient of the letter referred to the dissatisfaction with the Spanish government and predicted success if the disaffected were supported by the French people with any degree of spirit.

[26] East Florida Papers, vol. 26, Morphy to Nepomucena de Quesada, July 22, 1795 (transl.).

ment for the consul at Charleston, another change of direction in French foreign policy brought about his own relief.

Fauchet's successor Pierre Adet arrived at Philadelphia on June 13, 1795, and within two days assumed charge of France's Embassy. Adet's instructions from his government left him poorly equipped to face the political storm which was to burst in the United States soon after his arrival. The French Foreign Office had been silent as to what course he should take in the event of the ratification of Jay's Treaty. Indeed, his instructions differed only in minor details from those of his predecessor Fauchet: he was to honor American neutrality, agitate for adherence to the two treaties, especially those articles referring to the rights of French privateers in the ports of the United States, and he was to keep in close touch with the "French party."

Almost immediately upon assuming his duties he was confronted by urgent problems in the important consular district of Georgia and North and South Carolina in the form of the formidable dossier on consul Fonspertuis, charging him with misfeasance in office, a complete disregard of accounting for expenditures, and a scandalous public and private life.[27] The charges were so grave that although Adet possessed Fonspertuis' confirmation in his post, he felt that a replacement was essential. For the post, he chose young Victor Dupont, first secretary of the French Embassy, in spite of the fact that he did not have the power to make such an appointment. But if Adet thought Fonspertuis' replacement essential, the Florida adventure nonetheless retained its attractions.

Jay's treaty, which had been ratified by Congress on June 28, only awaited the President's signature; hence that part of Adet's instructions which called for him to exert every possible means to prevent the treaty from going into effect was a dead letter, and petitions such as that received from a "number of inhabitants of East Florida seeking aid in throwing off the Spanish yoke" [28] could be viewed in a new light. Dupont's departure for Charleston was delayed while Samuel Fulton, an American soldier of fortune who had been involved in the original expeditions, was commissioned to go to Florida and report back the prospects of reviving Genêt's old project.[29]

---

[27] *Correspondence of the French Ministers to the United States, 1791–1797*, pp. 760–761.
[28] Ibid., p. 828 (transl.). The petition was received by Adet on July 18.
[29] Ibid.

Fulton's report must have been highly encouraging. Adet carefully briefed young Dupont on how he was to proceed: he was to take advantage of every opportunity of reviving the expedition, but at the same time, the minister stressed, American neutrality was to be scrupulously respected. If the Florida affair assumed the character of an internal insurrection, he should favor it by sending aid. We are left to infer, however, that if the project necessitated an invasion, he was to steer clear of that, so as not to trespass on American neutrality. And if it turned out to be just another pirate operation, the minister wrote, he should not risk what feeble resources were available to him.

Before Adet's cautious instructions could be put into operation, however, and even before Dupont could arrive at Charleston, France's beachhead in East Florida was destroyed.[30] By July 17, Don Carlos Howard, commander of the Spanish Frontier Guards, drove Lang and Clark from their positions and forced them to take refuge across the Saint Marys River, on U. S. soil. Amelia Island held out until the two Spanish naval brigs *la Flecha* and *el San Antonio,* a gunboat, and a small privateer carrying troops from St. Augustine appeared before the port on August 2. The little flotilla opened fire at 7 p.m. The French filibusterers fled as precipitously as had the Spanish defenders before them and retreated across the Saint Marys, where they joined the small force assembled by Lang and Clark. At Newtown the leaders managed to hold together a semblance of organization until hopes of French aid finally evaporated.[31]

Dupont tried hard to sustain interest in the insurrection and went to great lengths to encourage the society members to assemble supplies on a larger scale than hitherto. The privateersmen, however, viewed his efforts with complete disinterest. "No one wished to board a vessel bound on an expedition that would not offer the lure of assured earnings such as privateering."[32] The hegira to the Caribbean had already begun. East Florida had lost its lure for the raiders. Charleston was of two minds as the privateers began to desert the port.

---

[30] On August 31, 1795, Fonspertuis was still awaiting the arrival of his relief (East Florida Papers, Fonspertuis to Diogo Morphy, August 31, 1795, transl.). Correspondence forwarded to St. Augustine detailing Franco-Spanish prisoner exchange.

[31] The *City Gazette,* August 25, 1795, also chronicled the debacle of the Florida insurrection.

[32] *Correspondence of the French Ministers to the United States, 1791–1797,* p. 829 (transl.).

5: JAY'S TREATY—THE GREAT BETRAYAL

The extent of the desertion of the port of Charleston by the French privateers was reported to the Governor of Florida by Don Diogo Morphy at the end of August 1795:

> All is quiet in Charleston and there is nothing to fear on the head of ship armings. The privateers going through this port are of small consequence. At the present only the brig *el Vengador de la Republica* [*le Vengeur*], Captain Carvin, of 16 guns is in port and it like the rest are experiencing manning difficulties; . . . for the moment all is quiet.[23]

The following tabulation, extracted from the columns of the *City Gazette*, records the entries of the raiders for the period between July 1795 and April 1796 and supports his observation.

Notice in City Gazette	Privateer Arrival	Prize Arrival	and Captor
July 2, 1795		*Britannia*	
		North Bay	*le Vengeur*
July 3	*le Vengeur*		
	Privateer schooner unidentified		
July 6	*l'Aigle*		
July 20	*le Vengeur*		
July 26		Schooner *Adventure*	*la Narbonnaise*
August 13		*Notre Dame de Rosier* (sic)	*la Parisienne*
October 5	*le Vengeur*	brig *Eliza*	*le Vengeur*
October 12	French schooner, 12 guns, unidentified		
October 20		*San Antonio de Almas*	*la Carmagnole*
October 21		ship *Rosina*	*la Carmagnole*
October 26	*la Carmagnole*		
November 10		2 Spanish schooners	*la Parisienne*
November 27	*le Vengeur*		
November 29		Spanish brig	*le Vengeur*
January 11, 1796	*le Brutus Français*		
February 12	*la Carmagnole*		
April 5		ship *Lymington*	*le Léo*
April 6		*Amity*	*le Léo*
April 7	*le Léo*		

---

[23] *East Florida Papers*, vol. 26, Morphy to Nepomucena de Quesada, Charleston, August 31, 1795 (transl.).

"Polacca [polacre] Brig at Anchor," a sketch by Sir William Symonds in his "Naval Costume," ca. 1837. The polacre, a Mediterranean rig, distinguished by long pole masts and lack of tops, was often seen in Caribbean waters at the end of the eighteenth century.

Thus, of the "regular frequenters" of Charleston, only *le Vengeur, la Carmagnole,* and *la Parisienne* continued to maintain a liaison with the port, to which they also dispatched a considerable number of their prizes. Soon after her arrival at the end of November *le Vengeur* disappeared. At some time in December she ran afoul of what was variously reported as a Letter of Marque and a British frigate among the Bahamas; heavily damaged after an engagement, she was either run ashore and set afire or blown up.[34] *La Parisienne* ended her career on a reef in the Bahamas (p. 84n). *La Carmagnole* also disappeared. What became of her is uncertain, although there is evidence that she became part of Victor Hugues' privateering fleet based on Guadeloupe.

By early November 1795, when French privateering had all but ceased, and rumors of a Franco-Spanish *rapprochement* had been gaining strength, Alexandre Bolchos appeared at Charleston in *la Parisienne* for the last time. He announced that a Spanish brig he had spoken reported that the English had declared war on Spain and that a sizable Spanish fleet had gone to sea from Havana. This news was confirmed on Tuesday, December 8, 1795, when the representatives of France and Spain at Charleston simultaneously revealed official copies of the treaty of peace between the two nations. The vessels of both Nations lying in the harbor displayed their colors united, and at noon fired a series of salutes.[35] The crews of French and Span-

---

[34] See *City Gazette*, April 14, 1795, and January 7, 1796.
[35] *City Gazette*, December 9, 1795.

"Ballahoe [balau, ballou, etc.] Schooner," a sketch by Sir William Symonds in his *"Naval Costume,"* ca. 1837. The balau was a distinctive West Indian type much favored by privateers during the period 1793–1815.

ish vessels exchanged visits and fraternization was accompanied with the usual numberless toasts.

If any French sentiment on behalf of a conquest of the Spanish Floridas had remained, it vanished. Not only did it appear that privateer havens and markets for the disposal of prizes would be opened in the Spanish possessions in North America for the use of French raiders, but the entire sweep of Spanish Caribbean islands from Puerto Rico to Cuba would throw open their ports, as would the whole of the Spanish Main. Indeed, Captain Silvestre of *la Carmagnole* had already sent one of his British prizes into Havana during a cruise which ended at Charleston on February 12, 1796,[36] and Benjamin Moodie in a letter to Vice-Admiral Murray, dated April 6, 1796, remarked that the coasts of Cuba already swarmed with French privateers.[37]

In relating to Murray the conditions of the port of Charleston, Moodie with cautious optimism observed that, "the lapse of time since any prizes were brought into port, gave me hopes that privateering was nearly at an end, so far as respected prizes being sent into this place . . .," but, referring to cases still pending before the Supreme Court, he nonetheless feared that decisions favorable to the privateersmen might yet see them return to Charleston and "encourage them anew in their depredatory plans."[38] His forebodings proved to be ill-founded; except for a few infrequent visits the French privateers never returned to Charleston. A new phase in the privateering war had commenced.

---

[36] *City Gazette*, February 13, 1796. This marked *la Carmagnole*'s last appearance at Charleston.
[37] BCC, p. 604.   [38] Ibid.

As we had noted earlier, Franco-American relations deteriorated rapidly toward the end of 1796. Jay's treaty was looked upon by France with deep bitterness as a betrayal of friendship and trust, and this was reflected in the attitude of her privateersmen in the Caribbean. Interruption of American shipping accelerated throughout 1797 as France entered upon a policy of countering British regulations on neutral rights with similar regulations of her own. Prize courts sprang up from Puerto Rico to Curaçao which, in the arbitrariness, corruption, and cynicism with which they treated American vessels brought in on a bewildering array of charges, many of which bordered on the frivolous, exceeded even the worst of Britain's colonial courts. As convenient symbols of American perfidy, American seamen bore the brunt of French resentment in acts of untoward violence and brutality.

France refused to negotiate outstanding differences as England had done in 1794. Conditions were set that were too unpalatable for the Federalist Government, which in March 1798 finally saved face by capitalizing on the "XYZ Affair" to engage in maritime counterreprisals against France.

The reprisals and counterreprisals were stopped by the Convention of Paris, signed on September 30 and ratified on December 19, 1800, which contained in article 24 an interesting but little mentioned provision:

> When ships of war of the contracting parties, or those belonging to their citizens, which are armed in war, shall be admitted to enter their prizes in the ports of either of the two parties, the said public or private ships, as well as their prizes, shall not be obliged to pay any duty either to the officers of the place, the judges or any others: Nor shall such prizes ... be arrested or seized, nor shall the officers of the place make examination concerning the lawfulness of such prizes; but they may hoist sail at any time, and depart, and carry their prizes to the places expressed in their commissions, which the commanders of such ships of war shall be obliged to show. It is always understood that the situation of the article shall not extend beyond the privileges of the most favored nation ....

France in essence had salvaged a part of the rights she had claimed during the days when her privateers were desperately seeking to maintain a foothold in the Western Hemisphere. Thus, when American privateers carried the burden of the war at sea during the War of 1812, French ports of refuge and French markets for the sale of British prizes contributed heavily to the maintenance of a cordon of American commerce raiders about the British Isles.

Chapter 6

THE PROFITS OF PRIVATEERING

IF THE PRIVATEERMEN'S PRESENCE HAD CAUSED inconvenience and apprehension to some citizens of Charleston, it was not without some positive benefit to them, for the economic upswing that Charleston experienced in the years 1793–1796 owed considerable to the presence of the French raiders.[1]

Although statistics concerning Charleston's overall trade during the period 1793–1796 are few and unreliable, fragmentary reports which appear in the *City Gazette* on February 13, 1795, and again on June 1, 1795, as well as other indicators, provide some foundation on which to base an estimate of the contribution of French privateering to the economy of the port of Charleston.

The figures published on February 13 give the sum of $3,869,021.49 as the value of foreign trade of South Carolina for the year October 1, 1793, to September 30, 1794. The figures, "highly gratifying to the citizen," which appeared on June 1, 1795, showed that for the six-month period from October 1794

---

[1] See TAYLOR "Wholesale Commodity Prices at Charleston, South Carolina 1732–1791," pp. 356–377, and "Wholesale Commodity Prices . . . 1796–1861," pp. 848–868. *Historical Statistics of the United States, Colonial Times to 1957*, supplies the following index for all commodities at Charleston for the years concerned herein (for 1792 to 1795 no statistics are available):

1790	97	1796	145	1799	133
1791	92	1797	122	1800	123
—	—	1798	129		

through March 1795 alone the total was $2,878,314.43, or an increase of 50 percent over the comparable period of the previous year.[2] In themselves, however, these isolated figures only suggest the extent to which the economy of Charleston as a port was affected. From the most cursory study of the newspaper columns of the same period one can find evidence of rising business activity in the increased space taken by merchants to advertise new lines of imported goods, both tropical and European, and in the appearance of new names and combinations of names among those of the old, established merchants. Beyond this, we feel the pulse of a city enjoying the fruits of prosperity in such newspaper items as announcements of horse-race meets, the attractions of Mr. Blanchard's spectacular exhibits, theatrical companies competing for the patronage of a play-going public, and the City Council struggling to regulate the swollen traffic in the streets.[3]

The published figures, moreover, do not take into account the value of the clandestine trade in guns, powder, shot, and, above all, in ships. Nor do they reflect the profits to Charleston's maritime industry from fitting out the raiders or to the legal profession for processing British, Spanish, and Dutch prizes. Neither do they give an idea of the profits to the shipchandlers who provisioned the raiders, to the owners of wharves where prizes were converted into raiders, to the newspapers that advertised the auctions of prize goods and prizes, and to the blacksmiths, whitesmiths, gunsmiths, shipwrights, sailmakers,

---

[2] It should be noted that the first set of figures include the 3-month inactivity caused by the embargo. Both sets of figures also include reexports. These, however, are not thought to have been of major significance in Charleston. For the first time in over three years an advertizement appeared in the *City Gazette* for April 21, 1795, indicating that the lumber trade, which ranked with rice and indigo as one of the prime export staples of South Carolina prior to the British restrictions of 1787, was enjoying a revival.

> Charleston Mills—Subscriber has received a large quantity of the best pine timber—also engages to prepare any quantity of *Particular Lumber* for the West Indies use such as windmill arms, points, beams, &c. . . . by having 6 or 8 weeks notice previous to arrival of vessels to carry them off. Ship Plank and Beams.

[3] Charleston's famous statue of William Pitt which had survived the American Revolution had to be removed from its site at the intersection at Broad and Meeting Streets, not because, as is usually held, that it was objected to by the "pro-Gallicans," but because it was a traffic hazard. Traffic had increased to such an extent that the *City Gazette* (January 15, 1795) published an appeal to the citizenry to keep to the driver's left at night: "This is the practise in all well regulated cities of Europe."

"English Merchant Schooner," a sketch by Sir William Symonds in his "Naval Costume," ca. 1837.

riggers, coopers, boatbuilders, ropewalkers, armorers, and the arsenal of other trades that shared in purveying to the needs of the French corsairs and vessel exporters.

Jean François Théric's "Etat Nominatif" (see appendix 1) which accompanied his memorial affords a rough gauge against which the privateers' contribution can be measured. He lists 72 prizes brought into Charleston alone during the period between Genêt's visit to that port in 1793 and his own departure for France in April 1795.[4] Of these, 52 can be identified as having been carried in during the period between the laying of the embargo and the closing of Théric's list. These prizes, for the most part the product of such captains and outfitters as Bouteille, Carvin, Hervieux, Peronne, Barre, and Garriscan, were valued at £114,985. Using the rate of exchange of 4s and 8d to the dollar,[5] the value in United States currency of the prizes taken amounts to $424,000, or about 14 percent of the value of all exports from Charleston for roughly the same period. For a truer measure, this figure should be augmented by the value of goods pilfered from cargoes by the privateersmen and their agents prior to evaluation of the prizes by the French consulate, and by the sizable amount, possibly another $200,000, of specie seized from various prizes.

---

[4] Excepted are those sent into Saint Domingue or Guadeloupe, as well as prizes still undergoing litigation at the time of his departure, such as *De Onzekeren* and *Somerset*.

[5] This rate is quoted in an advertisement for the sale of the British prize sloop *Betty Cathcart* taken by the privateer *Citoyen de Marseille*, Chabert (*City Gazette*, May 16, 1795).

Of the tentative net proceeds from prizes taken by the 38 privateers listed by Théric [6] (see Appendix 1) as operating out of Charleston between April 1793 and April 1795, 50 percent, or $312,000, represented the owners' share, the remainder being shared by captains, officers and crews.

Allowing the owners the generous average net profit of 30 percent, $218,000 would have been paid out for the services listed above, including a further small percentage of the net for consular fees.

There remains to account for the prize money that went into the pockets of captains, officers and seamen. If we assume that agents' fees and the spirit of thrift accounted for a reduction of 30 per cent of their share, a sum of $218,400 would remain to find its way into the tills and pockets of yet another sector of Charleston's business community, notably tavern, brothel, and boardinghouse keepers, as well as the theatres and slop shops. When we consider that the total free population of Charleston between 1794 and 1795 could not have been more than 17,000, a considerable amount of money per capita must have been put into circulation.[7]

Thus it might be more than coincidental that during the second half of 1796, well after the privateersmen had deserted Charleston as a permanent base of operations, the commodity index fell sharply, not to revive again until after 1800 when the rupture of the brief Peace of Amiens again plunged the western world into warfare which finally in 1812, engulfed the United States.

---

[6] Théric's Etat lists some 38 French privateers as regular frequenters of the port of Charleston. Of 3 of these, *le Petit Jacmel, le Violin* and *l'Enfant de la Patrie*, no record has been found at Charleston, and of the others, *la Guillotine, la Dorade, le Citoyen Français, l'Espérance, l'Intrépide* and *le Joujou National* called in at Charleston only from one to three times. The first three might have been the privateers noted by Théric as having sent their prizes into Wilmington, North Carolina. (See: Théric's *Memorial*, f 215.)

[7] Charleston, S.C., ranked as the fourth largest city in the United States, was considered as the sole urban area in South Carolina at this time. The following is extracted from U.S. BUREAU OF THE CENSUS, *Census of Population: 1950 . . .*, vol. 1, pp. 40–46 (Number of Inhabitants) (Washington, D.C.: Government Printing Office, 1952):

	Charleston, S.C.			Percent of Total Rural and Urban Population		
	Population	Increase				
		Number	Percent		U	R
1790	16,359	—	—	1790	6.6	93.4
1800	18,824	2,465	15.1	1800	5.4	94.6

Bibliography

MANUSCRIPTS

Benjamin Moodie letters. Public Records Office, London, PRO 133/FO 5–11.

"Les Capitaines & Armateurs des Corsaires Français en Rade de Charleston." Dated "12 Nivose de l'an 3eme [January 1, 1795]." Archives Nationalès, France, BB4, vol. 85, ff. 219–221.

"Copie de la Pétition addressée au citoyen Conssul [sic] par Garriscan, capitaine du navire Le Pichegru." Dated "Charleston, le 11 nivose L'an 3eme [December 31, 1794]." Archives National, France, BB4, vol. 85, ff. 222, 222 verso.

"Extracto de las ocurencias diarios de la escuadra del mando de tenientegeneral Don Gabriel Aristizabal." Museo Naval, Madrid, ms. 595, doc. 1, 268 pp.

East Florida Papers: Letters from the Governor of Florida to Captain General of Cuba, Florida, and Louisiana; correspondence with Ministers and Consuls. Library of Congress, Manuscript Division, vols. 24, box 49; 26[M2], boxes 51 and 52; 103 [L8], boxes 216 and 217.

Jean François Théric, négociant à Charlestown . . . au Ministre de la marine et des Colonies." Dated "5 frimaire [l']an 4 (26 9bre 1795)." Archives Nationales, France, BB4, vol. 85, ff. 212–216 verso. Cited as "Théric, Memorial." The Memorial and two of its attachments (cited as "Etat Nominatif") are translated in the Appendix.

"Etat nominatif et Produit net des Prises des Bâtimens Anglais, Espagnols & Hollandais . . . ." Ibid., ff. 215–215 verso.

"Etat nominatif des Bâtimens armés en cours sous le Pavillon de la République française . . . ." Ibid., ff. 216–216 verso.

Jefferson manuscripts. Massachusetts Historical Society, Boston, Mass.

"A journal of the Charleston Chamber of Commerce, commencing 6 of February, 1784." South Carolina Historical Society, (Charleston, S.C.), Manuscripts Collection.

Miscellaneous letters, 1789–1906, U.S. Department of State. U.S. National Archives, Record Group 59 (General Records of the Department of State).

Massachusetts District Court records, docket books, vol. 1, 1788–1799. U.S. National Archives, Record Group 21 (Records of the District Courts of the United States).

Order book, 30th Regiment, 7th Brigade, South Carolina Militia (Vanderhorst), 1793–1814. South Carolina Historical Society (Charleston, S.C.), Manuscript Collection.

Letters, "Rusticus" to "Gentleman." South Carolina Historical Society (Charleston, S.C.), Manuscript Collection.

NEWSPAPERS AND JOURNALS

[For details of titles and dates of publication, see Clarence S. Brigham, *History and Bibliography of American Newspapers, 1690–1820*. Worcester, Mass.: American Antiquarian Society, 1947.]

American Daily Advertiser (Philadelphia, Pa.), 1794–1796. Variously as *"Dunlap's . . . ," "Dunlap and Claypoole's . . . ,"* and *"Claypoole's American Daily Advertiser."*

Centinel (Boston, Mass.), 1793–1795.

The City Gazette & Daily Advertiser (Charleston, S.C.), 1793–1796. After January 1, 1795, as *"City Gazette & . . . ."* The files of the *City Gazette* in the Charleston Library Society, while the most complete in existence, lack copies for July 1 through October 5, 1795. This gap is in part filled by random copies in the library of the Wisconsin Historical Society, so that between the two sources it was possible to make a reasonably accurate survey of privateering activity.

Columbian Herald (Charleston, S.C.), 1794.

General Advertiser (Philadelphia, Pa.), 1794.

Georgia Gazette (Savannah, Ga.), 1793–1796.

Le Moniteur Universel (Paris).

New York Journal and Patriotic Register, 1793–1794.

State Gazette of South-Carolina (Charleston, S.C.), 1793.

South-Carolina State-Gazette & Timothy & Mason's Daily Advertiser (Charleston, S.C.), 1794–1795. Words of title variously arranged and punctuated.

PRINTED DOCUMENTS

American State Papers, Foreign Relations. Vols. 1, 3, 4. Washington, D.C., 1832+.

British counter case and papers, arbitration at Geneva. Correspondence respecting privateers fitted out at United States ports, 1793–1796. Printed by Order of the House of Representatives, 42d Congress, 2nd Session, 1871–1872. Cited as "BCC."

Correspondence of the French Ministers to the United States, 1791–1797. Frederick Jackson Turner, ed. (Seventh Report of the Historical Manuscripts Commission.) Vol. 2 of Annual Report of the American Historical Association for the Year 1903. Washington: U.S. Government Printing Office, 1904.

Instructions to the British Ministers to the United States, 1791–1812. Bernard Mayo, ed. Vol. 3 of Annual Report of the American Historical Association for the Year 1936. Washington: U.S. Government Printing Office, 1941.

The Mangourit Correspondence. Frederick Jackson Turner, ed. Vol. 2 of Annual Report of the American Historical Association for the Year 1897. Washington: U.S. Government Printing Office, 1898.

GENERAL

American State Trials. John D. Lawson, ed. 8 vols. St. Louis, 1914–1918.

BASSETT, J. M. *The Federalist System.* New York: Harpers, 1907.

BEE, THOMAS. *Reports of Cases Adjudged in the District Court of South Carolina.* Philadelphia, 1810.

BENTLEY, WILLIAM. *The Diary of William Bentley.* 3 vols. Salem, 1907.

CABON, ADOLPHE. *Histoire de Haiti.* Vols. 3, 4. Port-au-Prince, n.d.

CHAPELLE, HOWARD I. *The History of the American Sailing Navy.* New York: W. W. Norton & Co., 1949.

DALLAS, A. J. *Reports of Cases Ruled and Adjudged in the Several Courts of the United States, Philadelphia.* 3 vols. Philadelphia: 1799.

DE CONDE, ALEXANDER. *Entangling Alliances.* Durham, N.C., 1951.

FISCHER, DAVID HACKETT. *The Revolution of American Conservatism.* New York: Harper & Row, 1965.

FRASER, CHARLES. *Reminiscences of Charleston.* Charleston, S.C., 1854.

Historical Statistics of the United States, Colonial Times to 1957. Washington: U.S. Government Printing Office, 1960.

JAMES, W. J. *The Naval History of Great Britain.* 6 vols. London, 1841.

LECONTE, PIERRE. "Répertoire des navires de guerre français." Paris: Musées de la Marine, n.d. [Issued irregularly as a supplement to *Triton*].

JACKSON, MELVIN H. "The Consular Privateers." *The American Neptune,* vol. 22, no. 2 (April 1962), pp. 81–98.

MANGOURIT, MICHAEL ANGE BERNARD. *Mémoir.* Paris, 1795.

McMaster, John Bach. *A History of the People of the United States.* 6 vols. Boston, 1927–1929.

Moore, John Bassett. *International Adjudications.* 6 vols. New York, 1931.

Phillips, Ulrich B. "South Carolina Federalists. I." *American Historical Review*, vol. 14, no. 3 (April 1909), pp. 529–543.

———. "South Carolina Federalists. II." *American Historical Review*, vol. 14, no. 4 (July 1909), pp. 731–749.

Taylor, George Rogers. "Wholesale Commodity Prices at Charleston, S.C., 1796–1861." *Journal of Economic and Business History* (August 1932, Supplement), vol. 4, pp. 848–868.

Thomas, Ebenezer S. *Reminiscences of the Last Sixty-five Years.* 2 vols. Hartford, 1840.

Warren, Charles. *The Supreme Court in United States History.* 3 vols. Boston: Little Brown & Co., 1922.

Appendix

1. Memorial by Jean François Théric, Translated from the Manuscript Original (See Bibliography)

2. British, Spanish, and Dutch Prizes Brought into the Ports of Charleston, South Carolina, and Savannah, Georgia, between April 1793 and April 1796, by French Privateers based at or Frequenting Those Ports

Vu
1796 (frimaire an 4
26 9bre 1795)

Jean françois Théric négociant à Charlestown
Agent nommé et Envoyé auprès de la convention Nationale par
les Capitaines, officiers et hommes d'Équipages des Bâtimens, armés
En Course sous le Pavillon de la République française, étant de Relâche
au port du dit Charlestown, États-unis de l'Amérique.

212

Au Ministre de la marine et des Colonies.

Prises faites par nos Corsaires

Citoyen Ministre.

Tandis que le Courage françois triomphoit en Europe et de l'Intrigue
et du Nombre des Ennemis de la République, des Marins français, rassemblés
dans la Caroline du sud de l'Amérique, faisoient flotter avec honneur, le
Pavillon tricolor sur les mers des États-unis du Mexique et de
St. Domingue. le Craïon de l'Histoire tracera avec plaisir leurs succès,
et les dérobera à l'oubli, dont, jusqu'à ce jour, ils ont été Couvert aux yeux
de la France: ils ont rendu Célèbre à jamais le nom françois dans le
Nouveau monde.

C'est au Souvenir chéri de leur Patrie qu'ils ont Combattu, sous un autre
hémisphère, les Ennemis de la République: ils ont humilié L'Anglais
et L'Espagnol dans leurs Marines Royale et Commerçante; Et
L'émulation, qui fait les héros, a multiplié leur nombre.

L'Exemple fut donné par le Citoyen Jean Bouteille; Ce fut lui
qui arma le premier; Et les bâtimens armés en Course s'élevoient en
Germinal dernier, au nombre de trente huit ——: j'y joindrai à la
présente le tableau, et celui des prises faites par nos illustres Corsaires.
il prouvera que leur bravoure, excitée par l'Enthousiasme de la liberté, sembloit
aplanir les flots pour leur faciliter la prise, par abordage, des bâtimens
Ennemis.

Eux seuls ont porté des secours en vivres & en munitions de Guerre au
Général & à leurs Braves frères d'armes de St. Domingue. tel est l'usage
qu'ils ont fait en partie du fruit de leur Conquête.

Déjà, Citoyen Ministre, j'ai fourni, en leurs noms, Différens Mémoires
au Comité de salut public, Sections de la Marine, de la Guerre, et des
Relations Extérieures; Daignez en prendre Connoissance, vous jugerez avec
quel zèle ils ont servi leur patrie, malgré les Entraves que faisoit mettre la
faction Anglaise à leurs armemens. Tous en ont bien mérité.

Mais il en est parmi eux qui doivent plus particulièrement

fixer

1.

Memorial by Jean-François Théric

[The translator has endeavored to retain as far as possible the flavor of the manuscript original, a page of which is reproduced opposite, as it was composed by an eighteenth-century French businessman.]

Jean François Théric, businessman at Charlestown, Agent appointed and sent to the National Convention by the captains, officers and crews of vessels fitted out as privateers under the flag of the French Republic based at the port of the said Charlestown, United States of America,

To the Minister of the Marine and Colonies:

CITIZEN MINISTER:

While French courage triumphed in Europe over the numerous intriguing enemies of the Republic, some French seamen, gathered together in South Carolina of America, saw to it that the tricolor flew with honor over the seas of the United States, Mexico and Saint Domingue. History's pencil will trace with approbation their accomplishments and will shield them from the oblivion which until this day has concealed their deeds from the eyes of all France. They have made the French name redoubtable in the New World.

It is in the cherished memory of their country that they have fought, in another hemisphere, the enemies of the Republic. They have brought humiliation to the royal navies and merchant marines of the English and the Spanish, and the emulation which has made them heroes has multiplied their numbers.

The example was first set by Citizen Jean Bouteille. It was he who fitted out the first, and the vessels armed as privateers rose in Germinal last

[March-April] to the number of 38. I attach to the present a list of them (a), and of those prizes (b) taken by our illustrious privateers. It will prove that their gallantry, stimulated by enthusiasm for liberty, seemingly calmed the waves in order to facilitate their carrying of enemy vessels.

They alone transported provisions and war supplies to the General [Laveaux] and to their brave brothers-in-arms at Saint Domingue. Such was the use to which they devoted a portion of the fruits of their conquests.

Already, Citizen Minister, I have furnished various memorials in their names to the Committee of Public Safety, the Sections of the Navy and of War, and Foreign Affairs. Deign to look into them, and you can judge with what zeal these men have served their country in spite of the obstacles the English factions have put in their way in the fitting out [of their vessels]. All are most deserving.

But there are among them men who ought most particularly to be remarked by the government. I shall single them out.

CITIZEN JEAN BOUTEILLE, native of Narbonne, 55 years old, having lived for 15 years in Saint Domingue, where he was engaged in the coasting trade, purchased at le Cap a schooner that he named *la Sans Pareille*. On the very day that he learned of the declaration of war against England he fitted out his schooner with four swivels and shipped a crew of 37 men. On his first sortie he came upon a Spanish corvette with 20 gunports and mounting four guns and with a crew of 40, laden with the King's cargo. He boarded and captured her and sent her to Norfolk, where she has been sold.

Some time later he fell in with 4 English vessels, each of 500 tons, armed with cannon and laden with timber. He attacked them, and after a two-hour fight, captured them and took them to Charlestown.

He [Bouteille] is as generous as he is just. He recompenses all officers and men who behave well, and he gives bonuses to those who had the misfortune to have been wounded.

His patriotism is deep and sincere. It was he, in particular, who forwarded to the brave General Lavaux, at Port-de-Paix, supplies of food and munitions of war. He sent them at his own expense via several vessels, among them the Spanish [prize] schooner *la Seignorita*, Captain Goureau, and *la Narbonnaise*, armed with 12 guns, Captain François Hervieux.

Each time it was learned in the United States that the Republican armies had won some victory over its enemies, he gave, in order to stimulate patriotism, a sumptous banquet to which all the leaders of Charleton were invited, and at the end of the repast he had distributed to the poor of the place food, bread and money.

In Germinal last, having learned that 300 French seamen were being held prisoner at Havana, he arranged with a Spanish commissioner to ransom them for a new vessel, of 350 tons, named *Despillas* [sic] which he had taken from the Spanish.

Whatever the pleasure of rehearsing virtuous deeds, those of Citizen Bouteille are so frequent that it can be said of him that no day passes without his having done some good.

APPENDIX 1: THÉRIC MEMORIAL

I solicit for him, and in his name, the Brevet and Grade of *Capitaine de Vaisseau*.

CITIZEN JEAN-BAPTISTE CARVIN of Marseille, age 42, long-time mariner, Captain, at Saint Domingue.

Proofs of his courage and of his devotion to the French Republic are incontrovertibly established by the following deeds.

At the beginning of the war he bought and took command of the schooner *l'Industrie*, armed with 12 guns. At present he commands the brigantine *le Vengeur*, mounting 16 guns. He made several raids on the Spanish coasts [i.e., Puerto Rico, Santo Domingo, Cuba, and Florida]. He seized several vessels even in their very harbors. Among others he captured the Spanish brigantine *l'Aigle*, armed with 16 guns, and gave her to Captain Joseph Langlois of Missipi [Mississippi] to take into Charleston. En route he made a prize of a Spanish vessel called *Las tres Meranas* [*la Trasmerana*]. That vessel had as cargo 900 cases of cannon powder, weighing 300 pounds each, bound for Havana. Aware that General Lavaux lacked powder he sent it off to him immediately, and so as not to risk it all in a single vessel which might be captured at a single stroke by the enemy, he divided his shipment, in three and four thousand weights, among several vessels. All of them made port safely at Port-de-Paix.

General Lavaux, certain of Carvin's patriotism and courage, ordered him to come to Port-de-Paix with his flotilla of vessels, so that he might take command of a projected expedition against Montechristi, where warehouses of provisions were located that belonged to the Spanish of Saint Domingue and Fort Dauphin, this latter having been captured from the French [in January 1794].

Carvin obeyed the orders of General Lavaux [and took with him] all his vessels, which had been captured from the enemy, that is: *l'Industrie*, 12 guns; the brig *le Sans Culote*, 14 guns; the bateau *le Républicain*, 12 guns; and the schooner *la Carmagnole*, 6 guns. But unfortunately Carvin fell ill and remained so for two months. General Lavaux did not dare to confide the command of the flotilla to any one but its owner, and so the expedition was a failure.

I solicit also for him, and in his name, the Brevet and Grade of *Capitaine de Vaisseau*.

CITIZEN FRANÇOIS HERVIEUX, of Normandy, 28 years old, having resided 6 years at New Orleans, successively fitted out on his own account and commanded several privateers. At present he commands *le Ça Ira*, which belongs to him. He has taken several prizes, one of very great value. Although the [United States] Federal Government, against the letter and spirit of the Treaty of 1778, ordered him to turn over the major portion [of his prizes] to the enemy, his zeal has not slackened at all. Among other deeds that prove both his courage and his seamanship there should be cited the following: For two days he sailed in company with an English vessel of 24 9-pounders carrying a crew of 60 whites and 300 negroes bound for Havana. During this time he spied a favorable opportunity to attempt a boarding. In order to know the strength of the vessel he sent one of his officers with six men in a boat to ask for water and provisions [for his vessel]. The English Captain sent him some. The crew of the *le Ça Ira,* seeing the superiority of the Englishman, urged Hervieux to abandon his project. When the last man [of his crew] left the enemy vessel he fired a broadside into her while hoisting the flag of the French Republic.

I solicit for him, and in his name, the Brevet and Grade of *Lieutenant de Vaisseau.*

CITIZEN JOSEPH LANGLOIS of Missipi [Mississippi], 26 years old. It was he who, as I have said in the article on Carvin, while taking the prize *l'Aigle* to Charlestown, captured the Spanish vessel *las très Meranas* [*la Trasmerana*]. Since then he has commanded *la Mère Michelle,* armed with 18 guns. On his last cruise he took as prize and sent into Charlestown an English brig of 14 guns and another well-armed vessel of 500 tons also English. It was only through his great skill and only after several stubborn engagements that he took them.

I solicit for him, and in his name, the Brevet and Grade of *Lieutentant de Vaisseau.*

CITIZEN JEAN GAILLARD, of the Department of Angoulême, 44 years old, commanding the brigantine *le Général Lavaux,* armed with 18 guns. He shared constantly in the operations of Citizen Carvin in the capacity of chief officer. It was to him that the letter had entrusted the carrying of provisions to Port-de-Paix, and he eluded the enemy with great skill. In his last cruise he took by boarding the English vessel *Jamaica,* of 450 tons, armed with 22 9-pounder guns, laden with sugar and coffee, and two other vessels also richly ladened, but which had not yet entered Charlestown at the time of my departure.

I solicit for him, and in his name, the Brevet and Grade of *Lieutenant de Vaisseau.*

CITIZEN FRANÇOIS BAR of Bordeaux, 40 years old, commanding the privateer *le Courier National,* armed with 18 9-pounders. He formerly commanded the schooner *le Volcan,* of 10 guns. It was with that schooner that he succeeded in taking, after a fight of several hours, the vessel *le Courier National,* then called the *Courier of Liverpool.* This vessel, too, was richly laden.

I solicit for him, and in his name, the Brevet and Grade of *Lieutenant de Vaisseau.*

CITIZEN ALEXANDRE BOLCHOZ of Paris, 32 years old. He has commanded several vessels since the beginning of the war. At present he is owner of and commands the schooner *la Parisienne,* of 8 guns. He has taken prizes of the greatest value—all of them armed vessels. He captured an English brig armed with 14 guns which he sent into Charlestown. He engaged in a fight of several hours duration with *un* [word illegible], of 18 6-pounders. [When] the wind freshened he was forced to break off the fight, after he had killed many of the people on the enemy vessel and had inflicted an extraordinary amount of damage. On his side he lost his second gunner and a sailor. His chief officer Jean Fitter [?] of Bordeaux had his right arm shot off and he himself was seriously wounded in one arm. He was one of the first to carry munitions to General Lavaux.

APPENDIX 1: THÉRIC MEMORIAL

I solicit for him, and in his name, the Brevet and Grade of *Lieutenant de Vaisseau.*

CITIZEN CESAR PERONNE, 55 years old, from La Rochelle, commanding the brigantine *l'Aigle,* of 18 guns, he formerly commanded the bateau *le Républicain,* of 12 guns. He distinguished himself by making several raids on the coasts of Spain [Puerto Rico, etc.] where he captured several armed vessels and burned others.

I solicit for him, and in his name, the Brevet and Grade of *Lieutenant de Vaisseau.*

CITIZEN FRANÇOIS CHABERT of Marseille. He commanded with the greatest success the privateer named *le Citoyen de Marseille,* armed with 30 guns and a crew of 300. He took several heavily armed Dutch prizes and likewise took many English vessels, of which the major part are being detained by the Admiralty Court at Charlestown contrary to the terms of the treaty of 1778.

I solicit for him, and in his name, the Brevet and Grade of *Lieutenant de Vaisseau.*

Finally I solicit for CITIZEN GARISCAN confirmation of the rank of *Lieutenant de Vaisseau* provisionally conferred upon him by General Lavaux. I will not rehearse all the actions which have won him this rank. The General knows of them and has recompensed him.

CITIZEN MINISTER:

I have just named for you those seamen whose actions have won the most renown. But those who have fought under their orders, have equal right, by reason of their bravery, to advancement. It is the way to attach them more and more to the success of the arms of the French Republic; it is the way to assure [for France] the support and courage of more than 4,000 seamen dispersed among the different ports of the United States of America.

Salut et Fraternité

JOHN F. THÉRIC

Paris, 5 frimaire, an 4ᵉ de la
rép. française [November 26, 1795]

ÉTAT NOMINATIF

[Names doubtfully translated are marked with (?); for further identification, see Appendix 2. Discrepancies in addition and carry-over exist in the original.]

Number 1.

List of names and net proceeds from the sale of English, Spanish and Dutch prizes taken on the high seas of North America and the Antilles by the French seamen, Captains Jean Bouteille, Jean-Baptiste Carvin, François Hervieux, Joseph Langlois, Jean Gaillard, François Bar, Alexandre Bolchoz, César Peronne, François Charbert, and Gariscan, fitted out as privateers under the flag of the Republic of France and based at the port of Charlestown, United States of America, to wit:

English brig 4 Brothers	£ 662	19	5
English brig Morning Star	534	9	11
English vessel La Belle	1266	4	7
Brig Anna Magdalena	317	6	8
English brig Jessé	2014	15	6
English brig Providence	500	—	—
English ship 2 Brothers	1000	—	—
English brigantine Adventure	280	—	—
English ship Henriette	2000	—	—
English ship Souverain	2210	10	6
English brig Betsi	373	8	4
English brig Argot	280	—	—
English schooner Aurora	1053	11	—
English schooner Truro	1090	16	4
Spanish brigantine S$^{t.}$ Joseph	2318	14	4
English ship Friendship	9838	4	—
English schooner Minerve	936	2	4
English schooner Aurora	3838	18	9
Spanish vessel S$^{ta.}$ Isabella	318	18	1
Spanish schooner S$^{t.}$ Joseph	665	13	—
English schooner Hawk	760	—	—
Spanish schooner Ascension	2858	6	8
Spanish schooner Signora Del Carmel	530	12	4
Spanish polacre S$^{ta.}$ Yaimé [?]	7024	4	8
Spanish vessel Leon	886	12	4
Spanish schooner Las Dolores	858	10	—
Dutch brigantine Vrou. Chr. Magd. [?]	1200	—	—
English schooner Anne	374	11	2
English brigantine Suzanne	6901	14	2

APPENDIX 1: THÉRIC MEMORIAL

Spanish brig Del Sillaro [?]	4791	19	8
English ship Adventure	296	17	3
Spanish schooner S$^{t.}$ Joseph	540	—	—
Spanish ship Del Camino	10,090	12	11
English brig Nelly Carl. *[Caroline]	725	7	4
Spanish schooner Nostra Seignora	976	3	11
Spanish vessel Belinda	914	19	5
Carry over	£71,430	4	7
(Carry over	71,430	4	7)
Spanish polacre s$^{ta.}$ Tecla	8081	5	10
Spanish schooner Bonne Mere	1203	11	5
English ship Rambler	1190	—	—
English schooner Adventure	964	—	—
English ship Friendship	240	16	8
Spanish ship s$^{to.}$ Domingo / Spanish schooner s$^{t.}$ Joseph	2026	13	7
English ship Fanny	432	1	9
Spanish schooner s$^{ta.}$ Clara	180	13	11
English schooner Swallow	1664	17	5
English ship Smith	906	99	11
English brig Endeavour	8347	10	3
English brig Alerte	5961	2	6
English brig Fanny	5752	7	5
Spanish ship St. Joseph Desamel	303	17	3
English ship Courier de Liverpool	3053	16	5
Spanish polacre Sans Cayetano	7210	7	2½
Spanish brigantine Nostra S$^{na.}$ De las Dolores	6430	5	6
English schooner La Blonde	866	17	5
English brig Betsi	2000	—	—
English ship Brothers	263	12	9
Spanish schooner Dorada	470	17	9
Spanish ship S$^{t.}$ François	1778	6	5
Spanish schooner S$^{ta.}$ Maria	79	4	—
English ship Betzi	1400	—	—
Spanish schooner Louisiana	1161	13	11
Dutch ship Denoncekeron	1000	—	—
Spanish ship Parfaita	212	3	10
English brig Elisa	920	4	5
English ship Mermaïd	1800	9	3
English ship Tendre Mere	25600	—	—
English brig Trivoli	1600	9	6
English brig Favori	1200	4	—
Spanish brig Conception	20000	9	3
English ship Alfred	25000	18	4
English schooner Prosperité	920	6	—

{ These six prizes were unsold in Germinale, but they were estimated at these prices.

Total of two columns, 211,655   18   5½

Carried over	211,655	18	5½

To the proceeds of the prizes carried over must be added that of other prizes which entered port later, noting that at the time of my departure from Charlestown I was able to obtain only a summary of the proceeds without details.

There entered into the ports of Savannah and Wilmington forty prizes which yielded . .	165,000	. . . .	. . . .
There were taken into the ports of French colonies, Danish, and Swedish, thirty prizes which yielded	90,000	. . . .	. . . .
Finally there were burned at sea twenty five enemy vessels to the value of at least . . .	20,000	. . . .	. . . .
Prizes taken from our enemies, have produced to their loss, a total of 486,655£ 18ˢ 5½ᵈ	486,655	18	5½
This totals, in French money, seven millions seven hundred eighty six thousand four hundred ninety two livres, fifteen sols, four deniers	7,786,485	15	4

Observations

The vessel *L'Esperance*, belonging to Citizen Bouteille, had taken two Spanish prizes and one English: Captain Peyre brought these prizes to the Windward Islands. The constituted authorities [there] disposed of the major part of those prizes, doubtlessly for the service of the French republic. They were estimated to be worth four millions   4,000,000   . . . .

The total value of a large number of prizes brought into the northern ports of the United States at present cannot be given, the outfitters and captains not having been able to advise me of it before my departure. But these same will give at least   5,000,000   . . . .

Total	16,786,486	15	4

To the considerable losses that our privateers have inflicted on the enemies of the French Republic, must be added the loss of their seamen, a great number of whom have sought service in our vessels.

(signed) J.-F. Théric

APPENDIX 1: THÉRIC MEMORIAL

NUMBER 2.

List of vessels commissioned as privateers under the Flag of the French Republic according to Letters of Marque, some issued by the Commissioners, others by the Governor General of Saint Domingue, to several seamen, presently based at the port of Charlestown and others of the United States of America, to wit:

1. La Sans Pareille	4 swivels		20. Le General Lavaux	18 guns	
2. Le Genet [sic]	10 guns		21. Le Grand Port-de-Paix	12	"
3. Le Sans-Culote	12	"	22. Le Citoyen de Marseille	30	"
4. Le Vainqueur de la Bastille	4	"	23. L'Enfant de la Patrie	12	"
5. L'Industrie	2	"	24. Le Brutus	20	"
6. L'Atlante	8	"	25. L'Aigle	18	"
7. L'Ami de la Pointe-à-Pitre	12	"	26. Le Vengeur	16	"
8. La Montagne	14	"	27. Le Passe-Partout	12	"
9. La Minerve	10	"	28. Le Républicain	10	"
10. La Parisienne	8	"	29. Le Volcan	16	"
11. La Narbonnaise	10	"	30. La Carmagnole	8	"
12. L'Amour de la Liberté	12	"	31. Le Courier National	16	"
13. La Mère Michelle	12	"	32. La Guillotine	10	"
14. Le Qui Auroit Pensé à Ça	4	"	33. Le Jou-Jou National	4	"
			34. Le Violon	10	"
15. L'Esperance	14	"	35. La Dorade	12	"
16. L'Intrépide	14	"	36. L'Égalité	14	"
17. Le Sans-Culote	14	"	37. Le Petit Jau (?) Jacmel	4	"
18. Le Port-de-Paix	10	"			
19. La Révolution	12	"	38. La frégate le Dauphin	32	"

Observations

It is due to the example of success set by the schooners *la Sans-Pareille* and *l'Industrie* in capturing prizes from our enemies that this flotilla has been progressively formed. It has become even more redoubtable by the courage of its seamen rather than by the number of its vessels. It would have gained even greater success but for the fact that Captain Bouteille, although he purchased the frigate *le Dauphin,* could not obtain the free use of the vessel. Such is the strength of the English faction over the Government of the United States of America. But when France shall resolve to speak out and aid the brave seamen of the Republic with her authority the sooner will that influence disappear. Then Captain Bouteille will repossess his frigate, or rather it would be to the interests of the Republic to requisition the frigate for her service after first offering a just indemnity

"The Privateersman's Dream" watercolor by Pierre Ozanne, about 1798. On 14 December 1798 the 20-gun French corvette la Bayonnaise *attacked and captured the British 42-gun frigate* Ambuscade. *The picture shows the British frigate in the hands of the victors, her flag reversed, towing her heavily damaged captor at the end of a hawser. Courtesy Musée de la Marine, Palais de Chaillot, Paris.*

to Cit. Bouteille who would accept it at the first sign of interest on the part of the French Government. I will demonstrate the utility of this measure in a memoir that I will place before the Minister of the Navy.

(signed) J.-F. Théric

2.

British, Spanish, and Dutch Prizes Brought into the Ports of Charleston, South Carolina, and Savannah, Georgia, between April 1793 and April 1796, by French Privateers Based at or Frequenting Those Ports

The table of prizes is arranged alphabetically chiefly because dates of capture and the names of captors often have been unascertainable.

Errors in the names of the prizes caused by transliteration or purely phonetic spelling on the part of the reporters have been corrected in brackets directly following the name of the prize. Those names that have defied identification have been noted by question marks.

Valuations are in pounds sterling unless otherwise noted.

The information in the remarks column is derived from the sources noted, of which the following are abbreviated (see Bibliography for full title):

1. *The City Gazette and Daily Advertiser* of Charleston, S.C. (cited as C/G).
   The Georgia Gazette, of Savannah, Georgia (cited as G/G).
2. *British Counter Case and Papers, Arbitration at Geneva* (cited as BCC).
3. Théric Memorial, translated from the manuscript original in Appendix 1 (cited as Théric).
4. Bee, *Report of Cases* . . . (cited as Bee).

Spelling of names of prizes is derived from the first three, in the order given.

Footnotes are in remarks column.

Taken (17—)	Prize (Captain)	Rig and Flag	From →to Cargo	Captured by Privateer
July '95	Adventure (Elliot)	Schr. Brit.	New Providence→	la Narbonnaise
Aug. '94	Adventure (Mitchell)	Schr. Brit.	Nassau→ New Providence	le Qui-Auroit-Pense-à-Ça
May '94	Adventure (Griffith)	Sloop Brit.	Savannah→ Bahamas	la Sans Pareille, la Minerve
Sep. '93	Adventure (Cuzuenne)	Snow Brit.	Jamaica→ Norfolk	la Sans Pareille, l'Industrie
Oct. '94	Alert (Fullington)	Brig Brit.	Jamaica→ London 59 hhds., 8 tierces, & 52 bbls. sugar, 19 puncheons rum, 33 pipes Madeira, 30 bags coffee, 9 bags pimento, 4½ tons logwood	le Sans Culotte
Apr. '95	Alfred (Bryan)	Ship Brit.	Jamaica→ London Mahog. (logs & plank), sugar, indigo, coffee, pimento, cocoa, cotton, dyewood	le Brutus
Apr. '94	Ann* (Anderson)	Schr. Brit.	Jamaica→ New York	la Sans Pareille
July '93	Anna Magdalena	Brig Hamburg	—	la Sans Pareille
Apr. '94	Asuncion*	— Span.	Puerto Rico	la Montagne
Sep. '94	Atalanta	Ship Brit.	—	la Minerve
Oct. '93	Argo (Kingsley)	Brig Brit.	Jamaica→ Wilmington, N.C.	la Sans Pareille

APPENDIX 2: PRIZES, 1793—1796

Value (£) —Est. (BCC) —Sale pr. (BCC) —Net (Théric)			Remarks Notes on Other Columns	See text page
—			Taken near Crooked Island Passage, arrival at Charleston reported (C/G July 26, 1795).	96, 103
—			Arrival at Charleston reported (C/G Aug. 2, 1794).	
964	0	0		
500	1	1	Vessel and cargo advertized for sale (C/G Sept. 29, 1794); vessel reported not sold and in harbor on June 14, 1794 (BCC 612); reported bought by captors as store ship (BCC 614).	
—				
296	17	4		
1,200	0	0	Reported sold to "a Dane" (BCC 614); referred to as a brig in Théric's list.	14–17
—				
280	0	0		
800	0	0*	Arrival at Charleston reported (C/G Oct. 14, 1794). *Vessel and freight (BCC 618).	76n
—				
5,961	2	6		
30,000	0	0	Reported as run ashore entering Charleston harbor, later got off (C/G Apr. 8, 1795).	85, 85n
—				
25,000	8	4*	*Estimated, vessel reported as not sold February–March 1795.	
817	8	10	Arrival April 29 as prize at Charleston reported (C/G May 15, 1794); vessel registered at St. Johns, N.B., cleared for Boston after sale (BCC 612). *Théric's ANNE. †Vessel only.	43, 43n
66	10	0†		
374	11	2		
—			Arrival at Charleston reported (Philadelphia, American Daily Advertiser, Aug. 7, 1793).	16n
—				
317	6	8*	*Cargo only, vessel released as belonging to neutral.	
—			A 12-gun privateer, captured April 6 off Puerto Rico after 1½-hour fight (C/G May 16, 1794). *Théric's ASCENSION.	
—				
2,858	6	8		
—		—		28, 28n, 29, 42
233	6	8	Arrival of vessel reported (C/G Oct. 21, 1793); reported as bought by Thomas Stewart "for a Dane," cleared for Barcelona (BCC 612, 614).	17n
280	0	0		
280	0	0		

Taken (17—)	Prize (Captain)	Rig and Flag	From →to Cargo	Captured by Privateer
Dec. '93	Aurora (Dickie)	Schr. Brit.	Jamaica→ Charleston	L'Industrie
Feb. '94	Aurora (Dickie)	Schr. Brit.	New Providence →St. Augustine	la Sans Pareille
Nov. '94	Betsy* (Henderson)	Brig Brit.	Barbados	le Port-de-Paix (ex-le Vainqueur de la Bastille)
Nov. '94	Betsy (Williamson)	Brig Brit.	—	le Port-de-Paix
Feb.–Mar. '95	Betsy*	Ship Brit.	—	—
June '94	Belinda	Sloop Span.	—	la Narbonnaise
July '93	Belle* (Trott)	Sloop Brit.	Jamaica→ Charleston	le Vainqueur de la Bastille
Jan. '95	Betty Cathcart	Ship Brit.	Port-au-Prince→ Glasgow (See Remarks)	le Citoyen de Marseille
Nov. '94	Blonde	Schr. Brit.	—	le Patriote
July(?)'94	la Bonne Mère	Schr. Span.	—	—

APPENDIX 2: PRIZES, 1793-1796

Value (£) —Est. (BCC) —Sale pr. (BCC) —Net (Théric)			Remarks Notes on Other Columns	See text page
673 150 1,053	0 0 11	0 0* 0	Arrival of vessel at Charleston reported (C/G Dec. 1793); vessel purchased by Penman & Co. for the master, cleared for New Providence (BCC 612). *Vessel only.	17n
4,088 — 3,838	0 18	0 9	Arrival of vessel at Charleston reported (C/G Feb. 1794); vessel sold to "Smith of Boston," cleared for Boston (BCC 612, 614).	17n
— — 2,000	0	0	Libeled by British consul Moodie in December 1794 (BCC 591); libel dismissed with costs (G/G Apr. 2, 1795). *Théric's BETSI. Probably the same vessel as prize in next entry.	
—			Libeled by British consul as taken by illegally fitted privateer LE VAINQUEUR DE LA BASTILLE (BCC 591); decreed a lawful prize, case dismissed with costs (C/G Mar. 24 and 25, 1795. See also G/G (Apr. 2, 1795), *Williamson* vs. *Brig Betsy and J. P. Sarjeant* (Bee, 67–68), BCC (601).	15
— — 1,400	0	0	Noted as restored without damages in BCC (621, Moodie memorandum May 8, 1795). *Théric's BETZI.	
— — 914	19	5	Arrival at Charleston reported (C/G June 23, 1794).	
1,768 250 1,266	5 0 4	4 0† 7	Vessel bought by master, price included "negroes and some stores," reported as still in Charleston on June 14, 1794 (BCC 612, 614); arrived at Charleston July 19, 1793 (BCC 614). *Théric's LA BELLE. †Vessel only.	
—			Arrival reported (C/G Jan. 19, 1795); libeled "To be tried 20th March, if the commission sent to Philadelphia for the examination of witnesses returned by that time" (BCC 621); cargo itemized, sold by consent of parties, "the captors having appealed" (C/G May 16, 1795); Circuit Court found for captors (Bee, *Moodie* vs. *Betty Cathcart*, 292–299); Circuit Court upheld by Supreme Court (BCC 621);	
— — 866	17	5	Arrival at Charleston reported (C/G Nov. 28, 1794).	
— — 1,203	11	5	Théric list.	

Taken (17—)	Prize (Captain)	Rig and Flag	From →to Cargo	Captured by Privateer
June '94	Boyd (Frew)	Ship Brit.	Barbadoes→ London 78,000 ft. mahog., 21 tons dyewood	La Narbonnaise
Feb. '95	Brothers (Thomas)	Ship Brit.	St. Johns, N.S.→ Jamaica 14,000 ft. lumber, 40,000 shingles, 12,000 staves, 14 bbls. butter, 40 boxes spirit of turpentine, 20 bbls. oil, 31 hhds. stockfish 280 bbls. herring, 31 hhds. salmon (BCC 601)	Le Volcan (ex-Le Port-de-Paix)
Dec. '94	Caesar (Crosby)	Brig Brit.	Port-au-Prince→ Liverpool Coffee, sugar, cotton	La Parisienne
—	Camier (?) (Taylor)	Brig Brit.	—	—
May '94	Del Camino	Ship Span.	—	—
Sep. '95	Caseldea (?)	Sloop Span.	— 39,100 lbs. Spanish snuff, 1904 quintals tobacco, 108 quintals wax	L'Egalité
Mar. '95	Conception [La Concepcion]	Ship(?) Span.	—	—
Oct. '94	Courier* (Taylor)	Ship Brit.	— 140 bags cotton, rum, sugar	Le Port-de-Paix, Le Petit Port-de-Paix
Apr. '94	Las Dolores	Schr. Span.	—	—
Jan. '95	Dorada	Schr. Span.	—	—

APPENDIX 2: PRIZES, 1793-1796

133

Value (£) —Est. (BCC) —Sale pr. (BCC) —Net (Théric)	Remarks Notes on Other Columns	See text page
4,730 0 0* — —	Arrival at Charleston reported (C/G June 24, 1795); taken by whaleboats of LA NARBONNAISE, vessel and cargo recovered by British (BCC 594, 621). *Cargo 3,230, vessel 1,500 (BCC 594).	
3,000 0 0* — 263 12 9	Arrival at Charleston reported (C/G Feb. 27, 1795); vessel libeled, dismissed with costs (BCC 601, 621). See also *Benjamin Moodie* vs. *The Ship Brothers* (Bee, 76–78). *BCC (601).	
—	Arrival at Charleston reported (G/G Dec. 18, 1794); libel notice (G/G Jan. 22, 1795); libel dismissed (G/G Feb. 5, 1795); affirmed by Circuit Court (G/G May 7, 1795). Noted in BCC (621).	
—	Noted as having libel dismissed with costs (BCC 620); undoubtedly a misprint for COURIER, q.v.	
—	Théric list; see NOSTRA SIGNORA DEL CARMINO [NUESTRA SEÑORA DEL CAMINO].	
—	Libel notice, trial to be held at Augusta, Georgia, second Tuesday in November 1795 (G/G Sep. 10, 1795); Disposition not known.	
— — 20,000 9 3	Cargo and vessel advertised for sale (C/G Mar. 25, 1795); vessel unsold at time of departure of Théric in March–April, 1795.	
2,760 0 0† — 3,053 16 5	Arrival reported (C/G Oct. 24, 1795); offered for sale, vessel and cargo, (C/G Oct. 30, 1794); libeled by British consul, dismissed with costs (BCC 590). See also COURIER. *Théric's COURIER DE LIVERPOOL. †Cargo 2160/0/0, vessel 600/0/0. (BCC 594).	83, 83n
—	Théric list (SEE LA SIGNORA DE LAS —).	
— — 470 17 9	Vessel and cargo advertised for sale (C/G Feb. 4, 1795).	

Taken (17—)	Prize (Captain)	Rig and Flag	From →to Cargo	Captured by Privateer
Sep. '94	Eagle	Brig Brit.	Montego Bay	Le Républicain
Feb. '95	Eliza* (Francis)	Brig Brit.	Montego Bay	La Mère Michel
Oct. '95	Eliza	Brig Brit.	London→ New Providence dry goods	—
May '94	Elizabeth (Ross)	Ship Brit.	Jamaica→ London 285 hhds. sugar, 90 puncheons rum (G/G May 22,1794), 7 tons fustic (BCC 594)	L'Ami de la Pointe-à-Pitre, L'Ami de la Liberté
Mar. '94	Emanuel [Manuela(?)]	Sloop Span.	—	L'Industrie
Sep.(?)'94	Endeavour (Cummings)	Brig Brit.	Jamaica→ London 228 hhds. and 6 tierces of sugar, 5 puncheons of rum, 5 tons fustic	"Letter of Marque from Cayenne"
Dec. '94	Everton (Davis)	Brig Brit.	—	L'Egalité (ex-L'Ami de la Pointe-à-Pitre)
Oct. '94	Fancy*	Brig Brit.	—	L'Industrie
Aug. '94	Fanny (Long)	Sloop Brit.	Turk's Island→ Newfoundland	La Sans Pareille

APPENDIX 2: PRIZES, 1793-1796

Value (£) —Est. (BCC) —Sale pr. (BCC) —Net (Théric)			Remarks Notes on Other Columns	See text page
—			Arrival at Savannah reported (G/G Oct. 2, 1794); libel notice (G/G Dec. 4, 1794); auction of vessel and cargo advertized (C/G May 12, 1795).	77-78, 80-81
— — 920	4	5	Arrival reported (C/G Feb. 11, 1795); advertized (C/G Mar. 3, 1795); cargo and vessel advertized for sale (C/G Apr. 21, 1795). See also BCC (621). *Théric's ELISA.	
—			Arrival at Charleston reported (C/G Oct. 5, 1795); reference to letters aboard (C/G Oct. 9, 1795); sale of cargo advertized (C/G Nov. 4, 1795).	
13,500 11,183 —	18 1	1* 9	Bought by May, Hills and Woodbridge, resold to Messrs. Joseph Miller, McIver & Co., "Captain McIver has become a Danish as well as an American citizen," went to West Indies to get Danish papers (BCC 615); libel filed against vessel, also against Talbot and Ballard (G/G Oct. 16, 1794); decision on Elizabeth case: Ballard and Talbot to make good all damages and pay costs (G/G Dec. 25, 1794); decree of District Court upheld by Federal Circuit Court (G/G May 7, 1795). *Vessel valued at 2,200 (BCC 594).	57, 61, 96
—			Arrival at Savannah reported, cut out of Bay of Cuba (G/G Mar. 20, 1794); arrival at Charleston from Savannah reported (C/G Oct. 25, 1794).	40n
1,400 — 8,347	0 10	0* 3	*Vessel and freightage (BCC, 618).	
—			Libel filed against vessel, cargo and, £8,000 sterling (G/G Feb. 5, 1795); vessel and cargo restored by District Court to owners on Mar. 5 (G/G Mar. 12, 1795); Circuit Court affirmed decree of District Court (G/G May 7, 1795). See also BCC (621).	62n
— — 5,752	7	5	Arrival reported (C/G Oct. 15, 1794). *Théric's brig FANNY.	
2,000 — 432	0 1	0 9*	Taken August 14, 1794 (BCC 614); vessel and cargo advertized for sale (C/G Sep. 29, 1794). *Théric lists this vessel as a ship.	

Taken (17—)	Prize (Captain)	Rig and Flag	From →to Cargo	Captured by Privateer
Mar. '95	Favorite* (Grant)	Snow* Brit.	Jamaica→ Dublin 94 hhds., 9 tierces, 4 bbls. sugar; 65 tierces, 11 casks coffee; 120 bales cotton; 11 casks castor oil in bottles; a quantity of dyewood (BCC 601)	la Parisienne
May '94	Fortune Der Zee [Fortuin van de Zee]		—	l'Ami de la Liberté
Apr. '93	Four Brothers (Robb)	Brig Brit.	Nova Scotia→ Barbados	French National Frigate l'Embuscade
Aug. '94	Friendship (Stranack)	Ship Brit.	Jamaica→ Quebec 242 puncheons rum	la Montagne
Dec. '93	Friendship (Leslie)	Ship Brit.	Jamaica→ London	le Lascazas
Sep. '93	Grace (Brynan)	Schr. Brit.	Jamaica→ Philadelphia	la Sans Pareille
Apr. '94	Grenada Packet (Wemyss)	Ship Brit.	Pensacola→ London	l'Ami de la Pointe-à-Pitre
May '95	Hannah	Brig. Brit.	—	—
Feb. '95	Happy Return (Calvert)	Snow Brit.	—	—

APPENDIX 2: PRIZES, 1793-1796

Value (£) —Est. (BCC) —Sale pr. (BCC) —Net (Théric)			Remarks Notes on Other Columns	See text page
1,200	4	— — 0†	Arrival reported (C/G Mar. 25, 1795); vessel libeled by the British consul, libel dismissed with costs (Bee, *British Consul* v. *Schooner Favorite, and Alexander Bolchoz*, 39); decree affirmed by Circuit Court and by Supreme Court (BCC 621). *Théric's brig FAVORI. †Estimate; unsold March-April 1795.	
		—	Vessel boarded, released after captain and mate taken off, libel entered by captain; damages awarded (Bee, *Peter Martins* vs. *Edward Ballard and William Talbot*, 51-57).	57-59
2,092 380 662	19 6 19	9 8* 5	Noted in Théric's list as LE BROTHER, "bought by Penman & Co. for late master." Cleared for Jamaica (BCC, 612, 614, 614-15). *Vessel only.	
5,440 — 240	0 16	0* 8	Arrival reported (C/G Aug. 2, 1794); captain referred to vessel as MONTAGUE (BCC, 615); vessel and cargo advertized for sale (C/G Jan. 19, 1795); Circuit Court sent case back to District Court for reconsideration, "right to inquire into treaty" (BCC, 590); libel dismissed (Bee, *Stanwick* vs. *Ship Friendship*, 40-42). *Cargo 4,840, vessel 600 (BCC 616).	
17,644 435 9,838	18 0 4	9 0* 0	Purchased by H. Grant for owners, cleared for West Indies (BCC 615). *Vessel only.	27, 28, 29
350 —	0	0	Arrival of vessel reported (C/G Sept. 25, 1793); vessel reported sunk in harbor (BCC 612, 614).	
11,630 5,843 —	6 12	8 5	Notification of condemnation by office of French consulate (G/G Apr. 24, 1794); account of burning of GRENADA PACKET (G/G May 29, 1794).	55,55n, 57
		—	Advertized for sale at auction (C/G May 22, 1795).	
		—	Reference to capture by French privateer RESOLUTION [LA RÉVOLUTION(?)] (C/G Feb. 6, 1795); protest of captain, maltreatment, etc.; account of wreck of HAPPY RETURN, rescue of crew by Spanish schooner, capture of latter by LA SANS PAREILLE, plundered Americans set ashore on Cuba (C/G Mar. 30, 1795).	

Taken (17—)	Prize (Captain)	Rig and Flag	From →to Cargo	Captured by Privateer
Dec.(?)'94	Harcum	Schr. Brit.	—	le Port-de-Paix
Sep. '93	Harriet* (Strong)	Ship Brit.	Honduras→ London	la Sans Pareille, l'Industrie
Mar. '94	Hawk (Cocks)	Schr. Brit.	Jamaica→ Norfolk	l'Industrie
June '95	Hero	Ship Brit.	—	le Vengeur
Aug. '94	Isabel	Schr. Brit.(?)	—	l'Industrie
Feb. '95	Jamaica	Ship Brit.	—	le Général Laveaux, la Mère Michel
Oct. '95	James	Ship Brit.	—	—
July '93	Jessie*	Brig Brit.	Havana→ Baltimore 152 casks molasses, 24 boxes sugar, 30 hides, $529 specie	la Sans Pareille
Aug. '94	Jolly Bacchus (Cox)	Sloop Brit.	—	l'Industrie
Oct. '94	Judith (Cruikshank)	Snow Brit.	Montego Bay→ Londonderry 233 hhds. sugar, 50 puncheons rum, coffee, fustic, logwood, pimento, Madeira, mahog.	Little John (sic)
July '94	Juno	Schr. Brit.	Trinidad 317 boxes of sugar	l'Ami de la Liberté
July '95	Kingston	Brig Brit.	Jamaica	le Vengeur

APPENDIX 2: PRIZES, 1793-1796

Value (£) —Est. (BCC) —Sale pr. (BCC) —Net (Théric)			Remarks Notes on Other Columns	See text page
—			Libel filed (G/G Jan. 1, 1795); vessel and cargo returned to owners by District Court (G/G Jan. 15, 1795). See also BCC (621).	
5,769 2,000 2,000	19 0 0	6 0† 0	Arrival of vessel reported (C/G Sept. 15, 1793); vessel purchased by Thomas Morris, bought back by owners; sailed for Cadiz (BCC 612, 614). †Théric's HENRIETTE. *Vessel only.	17n
866 160 760	13 0 0	4 0* 0	Arrival of vessel at Charleston reported (C/G Mar. 1794); sold to "Karvint [Carvin], master of the privateer," reported still in harbor on June 14, 1794 (BCC, 612, 614). *Vessel only.	
—			Ran ashore on Isle of Pines June 15, set afire (G/G July 30, 1795).	87, 87n
—			Retaken by a British frigate off Stono, Georgia (C/G Sept. 23, 1794).	
—			"A valuable cargo" (C/G Feb. 10, 1795).	83n
—			Protest, including description of unidentified French privateer (C/G Oct. 30, 1795).	
— — 2,014	15	6	Arrival at Charleston and details (State Gazette of South Carolina, July 29, 1793). *Théric's brig JESSÉ.	16n
—			Prize reported (C/G Sept. 3, 1794); "taken by Captain Gallaspin [Garriscan] and carried into Wilmington, North Carolina" (BCC 614–615, 620).	
12,067 — —	0	0*	Arrival at Savannah reported (G/G Oct. 23, 1794); JUDITH and cargo libeled, privateer alleged as fitted out at Charleston (G/G Nov. 6, 1794); vessel returned to owners, circuit Court of Georgia upheld decree of District Court (G/G May 7, 1795); one half of cargo embezzled (BCC 591). *Cargo 9,567, vessel 2,500 (BCC 594).	
—			Arrival at Charleston reported (C/G July 17, 1794).	58
—			Arrival at Charleston reported (G/G July 16, 1795).	87n

Taken (17—)	Prize (Captain)	Rig and Flag	From →to Cargo	Captured by Privateer
Apr.(?)'94	Leon	Ship Span.	—	—
June '94	Long Island Packet	—	—	la Sans Pareille
Jan.(?)'95	Louisiana	Schr. Span.	—	—
Oct. '93	Maria	Brig Brit.	—	la Sans Pareille
Apr. '95	Marianne (Kinnear(?))	Schr. Brit.	Jamaica→ Virginia In ballast	le Général Laveaux
Mar. '95	Mary Ann (Knowland)	Schr. Brit.	Jamaica→	la Tendre Mère (Prize to le Général Laveaux)
Feb. '95	Mermaid (Clarke)	Ship Brit.	—	le Général Laveaux
Feb. '94	Minerva*	Schr. Brit.	—	l'Atalante
Apr. '93	Morning Star (Fullerton)	Brig Brit.	Jamaica→ Charleston	French National Frigate l'Ambuscade
Sep. '93	Nancy (Cooke)	Snow U.S.	Havana→ Charleston	le Jou Jou National
July '94	Nancy (Cooke)	Schr. Brit.	Bay of Honduras→	la Guillotine, la Montagne
Jan. 95	Nancy (Tatem)	Schr. Brit.	Bay of Honduras→ Jamaica	le Fonspertuis
June '94	Nelly Caroline (Otway)	Brig Brit.	Savannah→ Jamaica	l'Ami de la Pointe-à-Pitre

APPENDIX 2: PRIZES, 1793–1796

Value (£) —Est. (BCC) —Sale pr. (BCC) —Net (Théric)	Remarks Notes on Other Columns	See text page
886 12 4	Théric list.	
—	Recaptured by British privateer, FLYING FISH (G/G July 10, 1794).	60
—	Théric list.	
— 1,161 13 11		
—	Arrival at Charleston reported (New York Journal and Patriotic Register, Oct. 16, 1793); not mentioned in Théric or BCC.	17n
—	Vessel libeled, British consul Moodie noted that cost of proceedings did not warrant it (BCC 601).	
—	Arrival at Charleston reported, "afterwards given up to her owners" (C/G Mar. 2, 1795).	
— — 1,800 9 3*	Advertizement of monition to appear in Federal District Court (C/G Mar. 3, 1795); decision of Court appealed by British Consul (BCC 602). See also Bee (69–73).	70,83n
	*Estimated; vessel not sold, March–April 1795.	
— — 936 2 4	Arrival at Charleston and details (South Carolina State Gazette, Jan. 5, 1795). *Théric's MINERVE.	28,28n
800 2 0 212 6 8* 534 9 11	"Bought by Penman & Co. for late master," cleared for Jamaica (BCC 612, 614). *Vessel only.	
—	Vessel seized on suspicion of being enemy property, plundered of $12,000 in specie, court found for plaintiff, levied damages of $12,000 against privateer, plus costs (Bee, *Thomas Tunno* vs. *Benedict Preary*, 6–8).	
—	Arrival at Tybee Roads reported (G/G Aug. 2, 1794); advertizement by French consulate for claims against prize (G/G Aug. 14, 1794).	
—	Vessel libeled by British consul, returned after cargo plundered (BCC 602; Bee, *British Consul* vs. *Schooner Nancy et al.*, 73–74). See also BCC (621).	
2,030 5 9 — 725 7 4	Listed as not sold by June 14, 1794 (BCC 612); listed by Théric as NELLY CARL. [CAROLINE].	

141

Taken (17—)	PRIZE (Captain)	Rig and Flag	From →to Cargo	Captured by PRIVATEER
Jan. '95	NOSTRA SEIGNORA DE LOS DOLORS [NUESTRA SEÑORA DE LOS DOLORES]	Brigtn. Span.	—	—
May '94	NOSTRA SIGNORA DEL CARMINO* [NUESTRA SEÑORA DEL CAMINO]	Ship Span.	Cuba→Spain "a very valuable cargo"	LA MINERVE
Apr. '95	NUESTRA SEÑORA DEL CARMEN	Polacre Span.	Barcelona→	LE BRUTUS
June '94	NOSTRA SEIGNORA	Schr. Span.	—	—
Jan. '95	DEN ONZEKEN [DE ONZEKEREN]	Ship Dutch	Demerara→ London	LE CITOYEN DE MARSEILLE
Jan.–Feb.(?)'95	PARFAITA(?)	— Span.	—	—
Apr. '95	PELOR (Brian)	— Brit.	—	—
Apr. '95	PHOEBE (Andrews)	Ship Brit.	Montego Bay→ Liverpool "valuable cargo, rum, sugar, coffee, cotton"	LA MÈRE MICHEL
Feb. '95	PHYA [PHYN]	Ship Brit.	—	LE GÉNÉRAL LAVEAUX
Nov. '95	POLLY (Savage)	Schr. Brit.	New Orleans→ Baltimore	L'EGALITÉ
July '94	POLLY (Wright)	Sloop U.S.	Charleston→ New Providence	LA NARBONNAISE
July '95	POLLY	Schr. (?)	New Brunswick→	LA NARBONNAISE

APPENDIX 2: PRIZES, 1793—1796 143

Value (£) —Est. (BCC) —Sale pr. (BCC) —Net (Théric)			Remarks Notes on Other Columns	See text page
— — 6,430	5	6	Cargo and vessel advertized for sale (C/G Feb. 4, 1795); reported in Théric as Nuestra Sra. de las Dolores.	
— — 10,090	7	11	Cargo and vessel advertized for sale (C/G Sep. 29, 1794); vessel libeled, libel dismissed with costs (Bee, *Don Josiah Salderondo* vs. *Ship Nostra Signora del Camino, and Hervieux et al.*, 43–47). *Théric's Del Camino(?).	
—			Arrival at Savannah reported (G/G Apr. 9, 1795; C/G Apr. 16, 1795).	
— — 976	3	11	Théric list.	
— — 1,000	0	0	Arrival at Charleston reported, "said to be Dutch" (C/G Jan. 20, 1795); cargo and vessel advertized for sale (C/G May 14, 1795); mentioned as Dinon Zecheron (BCC 600); reported in Théric as Denoncekeron.	
— — 212	3	10	Théric list.	
—			Advertizement of sale of cargo and vessel (C/G Apr. 21, 1795).	
—			Arrival at Charleston May 2, 1795, reported, account of engagement, first and second mates and two men killed, almost all men wounded (G/G May 7, 1795).	
—			Libeled by British consul (BCC 621); monition advertized for March 12 (C/G Mar. 3, 1795).	
—			Advertizement of libel against vessel, *John Savage* vs. *Polly* and privateer *Egalité*; vessel plundered of 36 barrels containing $10,978 "and a half dollar" in silver, also a trunk of plate, $158 from "one Mrs. Freeman"; trial set for Dec. 19, 1795 (G/G Dec. 12, 1795). Disposition not known.	
—			Carried to Port-de-Paix, there ruled to be illegal seizure by Court of Admiralty, vessel ran ashore before redelivery to Wright, suit brought for damages, damages awarded (Bee, *M'Grath* vs. *Sloop Candalaro and Henri Hervieux*, 60–65).	
—			Sailed July 5, 1795, taken same day (C/G July 26, 1795). Vessel probably that of next entry.	

Taken (17—)	Prize (Captain)	Rig and Flag	From →to Cargo	Captured by Privateer
July '95	Polly (Prince)	Schr. (?)	Mole St. Nicholas, Haiti→ Charleston	la Narbonnaise
July '95	Potowmac	Brig Brit.	Jamaica→	le Vengeur
Nov. '94	Princess of Asturias [la Princesa de Asturias]	Brig Brit.	Cuba→	le Républicain
June '94	Prosperity* (Kelley)	Schr. Brit.	Jamaica→ Shelburne N.S. 28 puncheons rum, 2 hhds. sugar, 5 hhds. molasses, 6 bales cotton, 1,500 lbs. coffee, $1,636 in specie	la Parisienne
Sep. '93	Providence (Shoesmith)	Brig Brit.	Honduras→ Jersey	la Sans Pareille
June '94	Ragel(?)	—	—	la Parisienne
July '94	Rambler	Sloop Brit.	Harbour Island →Abaco 5 negroes	l'Ami de la Liberté
Oct. '95	Rosina	Ship Brit.	Jamaica→ 30 bales dry goods	la Carmagnole
Sep. '95	Sacra Familia	Ship Brit.	La Guayra→ Indigo, cocoa, tar, cotton	le Général Laveaux
Oct. '95	San Antonie des Almas [San Antonio de las Almas(?)]	— Span.	—	la Carmagnole
Oct. '94 to Jan. '95	San Cayetano	Polacre Span.	—	—

APPENDIX 2: PRIZES, 1793–1796　　　　　　　　　　　　　　　　　　　　　145

Value (£) —Est. (BCC) —Sale pr. (BCC) —Net (Théric)	Remarks Notes on Other Columns	See text page
—	Taken mid-July, vessel owned by Messrs. Penman & Co., Hary (sic) Grant and John Price of Charleston, arrived Charleston July 22, outrages of prize crew reported (C/G July 26, 1795).	
—	Arrival at Charleston reported (G/G July 16, 1795).	
—	Arrival at Charleston reported (C/G Nov. 18, 1794); referred to as being converted to French privateer (BCC 603).	
1,155　0　0 — 920　6　0	Arrival at Charleston reported (C/G June 30, 1794); listed among vessel taken by Charleston privateers (BCC 614); vessel libeled by the British consul as captured by illegal privateer, formerly the American schooner HAWK (Bee, *Kelley, Jun.* vs. *Schooner Prosperity and Cargo, and John Cooke*, 38–39); vessel restored with damages (BCC 614, 621). *Théric's PROSPERITIÉ.	
1,699　1　4 550　0　0* 500　0　0	Vessel and cargo bought by William Dicker (or Decker) and cleared for New York (BCC 612, 614); arrival of vessel reported (C/G Sept. 14, 1793). *Vessel only.	
—	Arrival at Charleston reported (C/G Jun. 8, 1794).	
396　13　4 — 1,190　0　0	Vessel libeled by British consul Moodie, restored as taken by illegal privateer with damages (BCC 614, 616, 621). See also *Teasdale* vs. *Sloop Rambler and Cargo and Edward Ballard* (Bee, 9–11).	
—	Arrival at Charleston reported, captured on "northside of Jamaica" (C/G Oct. 22, 1795).	
—	Arrival at Charleston September 23, 1795, reported, taken on September 7 off Puerto Rico (G/G Oct. 1, 1795).	
—	Arrival at Charleston reported, taken on the coast of Cuba after ¾-hour engagement, armed with 8 carriage guns (C/G Oct. 22, 1795).	
—	Théric list.	
7,210　7　2½		

Taken (17—)	Prize (Captain)	Rig and Flag	From →to Cargo	Captured by Privateer
Nov. '94	Santa Caterina [Santa Catalina]	Polacre Span.	— Red & white wine, vinegar, brandy, salad oil, variety dry goods, 40 elephant teeth, anchovies	le Port-de-Paix
Mar. '95	Santa Clara	Schr. Span.	Havana→	la Parisienne
Feb. '95	Santa Maria	Schr. Span.	Havana→ Port-Au-Prince	l'Egalité
May '94	St. Joseph* [San José?]	Schr. Span.	—	la Montagne
Sep. '93	St. Joseph [San José?] (Castello)	Brigtn. Span.	Cartagena de Las Indias→Spain	la Sans Pareille
May '94	St. Joseph [San José]	Schr. Span.	—	la Parisienne
Sep.–Oct.(?)'94	St. Joseph Desamel(?)	Ship Span.	—	—
June '94	St. Mary [Santa Maria]	Schr. Span.	Havana→	—
Aug. '94	Sta. Clara* [Santa Clara]	— Span.	—	la Parisienne
Jan.(?)'94	Sta. Isabella [Santa Isabella]	Ship Span.	—	—
July '94	Sta. Tecla	Polacre Span.	—	—
Apr. '95	Santo Christo de la Caridad	— Span.	Montechristi→ Havana	le Brutus
July '94	St. Catherine [Santa Catalina]	— Span.	—	l'Ami de la Liberté

APPENDIX 2: PRIZES, 1793–1796

Value (£) —Est. (BCC) —Sale pr. (BCC) —Net (Théric)	Remarks Notes on Other Columns	See text page
—	Arrival at Charleston reported, taken off Puerto Rico (C/G Nov. 24, 1795); referred to as SAUNZE CARATANA (sic) (C/G Nov. 27, 1794); advertizement of sale of remainder of cargo of the polacre SANTA CALTANA (sic) (C/G Dec. 3, 1794).	
—	Arrival at Charleston reported (C/G Mar. 12, 1795).	
— — 79 4 0	Arrival at Charleston reported (C/G Feb. 28, 1795).	
— — 540 0 0	Taken off St. Augustine, Fla. (C/G May 18, 1794). *Possibly the second schooner ST. JOSEPH of Théric's list.	
— — 2,318 14 4	ST. JOSEPH featured in case of *Castello* vs. *Bouteille*, alleged to have been originally captured by VAINQUEUR DE LA BASTILLE (ex-FAIR MARGARET), libel dismissed (Bee, 29–34).	
— — 2,026 13 7*	Théric list. *Théric's valuation included schooner ST. DOMINGO, q.v.	
— — 303 17 3	Théric list.	
—	Arrival at Charleston reported (C/G June 23, 1794).	
— — 180 13 11	Arrival at Charleston reported, vessel taken in St. Marc (British occupied St. Domingue) (C/G Sep. 9, 1794). *Possibly Théric's STA. CLARA.	
— — 318 18 1	Théric list.	
— — 8,081 5 10	Théric list.	
—	Arrival at Savannah reported (G/G Apr. 9, 1795; C/G Apr. 16, 1795).	
—	Arrival at Charleston reported (C/G July 11, 1794).	

Taken (17—)	Prize (Captain)	Rig and Flag	From →to Cargo	Captured by Privateer
Nov. '95	St. Christ de Montealvair [Santo Christo de Monte Alvaro?]	— Span.	Malaga→ Havana Wine and fruit	le Vengeur
May '94	St. Domingo [Santo Domingo]	Schr. Span.	— Sugar, hides, soap, cordage, etc.	la Parisienne
Dec. '94	St. Francis* [San Francisco] (Xavier)	Ship Span.	Jamaica→Cuba 26 negroes, trunk of dry goods	le Républicain, la Révolution
Apr. '94	St. Jago*	Polacre-Brig Span.	Barcelona→ Wine, fruit, brandy	la Montagne
Apr. '94	Signor del Car--* [Nuestra Señora del Carmen?]	Schr. Span.	—	—
Apr. '94	la Signora de las - - - - - - - [Nuestra Senora de las Dolores?]*	Schr. Span.	—	la Sans Pareille
—	la Signoria(?)	—	—	l'Industrie(?)
Apr. '94	del Sillaro(?)	Brig Span.	—	—
July '94	Sinteric(?)	Schr. Span.	—	la Guillotine, la Montagne
July '94	Smith	Sloop Brit.	—	la Parisienne
Oct. '94	Somerset (Ormond)	Brig. Brit.	—	l'Ami de la Pointe-à-Pitre

APPENDIX 2: PRIZES, 1793-1796

Value (£) —Est. (BCC) —Sale pr. (BCC) —Net (Théric)	Remarks Notes on Other Columns	See text page
—	Arrival at Charleston November 30, 1795, reported; captured on November 8 (G/G Dec. 10, 1795).	
— — 2,026 13 7*	Arrival at Charleston reported (G/G May 28, 1795). *Théric's valuation included schooner ST. JOSEPH, q.v.	
— — 1,778 6 5	Arrival in January of "FRANCISCO" reported (G/C Jan. 15, 1795); advertizement for sale of vessel and cargo, 10 guns, 4 swivels, "together with all her warlike stores" (C/G Jan. 20, 1795). *Théric's ST. FRANÇOIS.	
— — 7,024 4 8	Arrival at Charleston April 18 reported, cargo valued at $150,000 (G/G May 1, 1795). *Possibly Théric's STA. JAIME.	
— — 530 12 4	Arrival at Charleston April 19, 1794, reported (G/G May 1, 1794). *Probably Théric's Spanish schooner SIGNORA DEL CARMEL.	
— — 858 10 0	Arrival at Charleston April 23, 1794, reported (G/G May 1, 1794). *Probably Théric's Spanish schooner LAS DOLORES.	
— — 4,791 19 8	Captured by Captain Carvin (BCC 601). Théric list.	
— — 8,081 5 10	Arrival at Savannah reported (G/G Aug. 7, 1794), advertizement by French consulate for claims against prize (G/G Aug. 11, 1794).	
— — 906 9 11	Théric list.	
—	Arrival at Frederica, Ga., reported (C/G Oct. 15, 1794); libel filed in District Court of Georgia against vessel and Ballard for "piratical seizure" (G/G Nov. 6, 1794); vessel restored with cargo to owners (G/G Jan. 15, 1795); "run away with by captors, and the cargo landed and sold at St. Mary's, about 390 bales of cotton, part of the cargo, had been recovered" (BCC 620); Circuit Court affirmed decree of lower court in *James Ormond* vs. *Brig Somerset* (G/G May 7, 1795).	

Taken (17—)	Prize (Captain)	Rig and Flag	From →to Cargo	Captured by Privateer
Sep. '93	Sovereign (Brown)	Ship Brit.	Honduras→ London	la Sans Pareille, l'Industrie
Apr. '94	Susannah* (McIsaac)	Brig. Brit.	Jamaica→ London	la Sans Pareille
Sep. '94	Swallow (Johnson)	Schr. Brit.	— Herring, 2 Negroes	la Parisienne
Feb. '95	la Tendre Mère	Ship Brit.	Port-Au-Prince→ Sugar, cotton, coffee, indigo	le Général Laveaux
Mar. '95	Tiroli [Tivoli] (Barclay)	Brig Brit.	Kingston→ 1013 bales cotton, 5 hhds., 1 tierce sugar, logwood, and mahog.	la Mère Michel
Sep. '94	Tres Meronas [la Trasmerana] (Trabadna)	—	Vera Cruz→ Havana 842 boxes of gun powder (150 lbs. each), pease, beans, lead, logwood, dried meat, $4,242 in specie, guns, ball	le Républicain
Oct. '93	Truro	Schr. Brit.	Jamaica→ New Brunswick	l'Industrie

APPENDIX 2: PRIZES, 1793–1796

Value (£) —Est. (BCC) —Sale pr. (BCC) —Net (Théric)	Remarks Notes on Other Columns	See text page
7,731 10 0 500 0 0* 2,210 10 6	Arrival of vessel reported (C/G Sept. 15, 1793); vessel bought by Thomas Stewart for owners, in harbor June 14, 1794, cleared for Cadiz by November 1794 (BCC 612, 614).	
12,358 10 3 — 6,901 14 2	Arrival April 28, 1794, at Charleston, reported; SUSANNAH, ex-HARRIET, owned by Abraham Sasportas, was taken to Jamaica; there condemned as a prize, sold to British owners, and sent to sea as SUSANNAH; later sold for £163/0/0, reported still in Charleston on July 14, 1794 (BCC 612–613). *Théric's brigantine SUZANNE.	
1,500 0 0 — 1,664 17 5	Arrival reported at Charleston, taken to St. Domingue (C/G Sept. 9, 1794); vessel and cargo advertized for sale (C/G Sept. 17, 1794); libel against vessel dismissed, vessel valued at £1,200, negroes at £140, herrings at £140 (BCC 594, 619). SWALLOW was apparently bought for a privateer and left Charleston in late November; reported as taking a British vessel (C/G Jan. 7, 1795); reported by British consul at Charleston as fitting out as a privateer (BCC 593).	
— — 25,600 0 0*	Arrival at Charleston reported (C/G Feb. 16, 1795); prize captured British schooner MARY ANN (q.v.); prize not sold by March–April 1795 (Théric). *Estimated.	
9,000 0 0* — 1,600 9 6†	Arrival at Charleston reported (C/G Mar. 27, 1795); mentioned by Théric as not sold by March–April 1795; vessel libeled by British consul Moodie (BCC 601). *Vessel only. †Estimated.	
—	Arrival at Savannah with EAGLE reported (G/G Oct. 2, 1794); libel filed against vessel and cargo Dec. 2 (G/G Dec. 4, 1794); Georgia District Court gave decree against libelants of vessel and EAGLE (G/G Jan. 8, 1795); appeal against decree of District Court withdrawn (G/G May 7, 1795).	
— 1,369 12 9 1,090 16 4	Vessel reported to have been brought into Savannah, she was bought by Carvin and sent to Charleston. John Wallace, British consul at Savannah, noted that vessel and cargo were sold before he had received "any instructions from the consul-general [Phineas Bond] respecting valuation" (BCC 614).	

Taken (17—)	Prize (Captain)	Rig and Flag	From →to Cargo	Captured by Privateer
Sep. '93	Two Brothers (Woodman)	Bark Br.	Honduras→ Liverpool	la Sans Pareille, l'Industrie
Dec. '94	Vere	Ship Brit.	—	(See remarks)
May '94	Vrouw Christina Magdalena*	Brigtn. Dutch	Curacao→ Amsterdam	l'Ami de la Pointe-à-Pitre

UNIDENTIFIED

Taken (17—)	Prize	Rig and Flag	From →to Cargo	Captured by Privateer
Oct. '94	—	Brig. Span.	Havana→ Indigo, etc.	le Républicain
Nov. '94	—	—	—	l'Ami de la Pointe-à-Pitre
Dec. '94	—	Schr.(?)	"from Savana"	le Port-de-Paix
Jan. '95	—	Sloop Span.	—	le Républicain
Jan. '95	—	Sloop Brit.(?)	New Providence→	la Parisienne
Jan. '95	—	Sloop Span.	—	l'Ami de la Liberté
Feb. '95	—	Brig Brit.	—	la Mère Michel
Nov. '95	—	Schr. Span.	—	la Parisienne
Nov. '95	—	Schr. Span.	—	la Parisienne
Nov. '95	—	Brig. Span.	—	le Vengeur
Jan. '95	—	Schr.	Jamaica→ New Orleans	le Qui-Auroit-Pensé-à-Ça
Jan. '95	—	Schr.	—	le Fonspertuis

APPENDIX 2: PRIZES, 1793–1796

Value (£) —Est. (BCC) —Sale pr. (BCC) —Net (Théric)	Remarks Notes on Other Columns	See text page
4,266 16 6 1,000 0 0* 1,000 0 0	Arrival of vessel reported (C/G Sept. 16, 1793); vessel purchased by Thayer & Bartleu Co., cleared for Providence, R.I. (BCC 612, 614). *Vessel only.	
—	About December 1, the vessel was captured by 200 French prisoners who rose and ran her ashore on the coast of Georgia; account of rising and difficulties of getting American assistance (BCC 621); libel filed by master before District Court of South Carolina for part of stores etc.; case dismissed on plea to jurisdiction (Bee, *Reid* vs. *Ship Vere*, 66–67).	
— — 1,200 0 0	*Joost Jansen* vs. *Brigantine Vrow Cristina Magdelena and Edward Ballard* (libel claimed illegal capture), decision reported (C/G Aug. 9, 1794); cargo advertized for sale (C/G Sep. 30, 1794). *Théric's "Vrouw. Chr. Magd."	

PRIZES

—	Reported entering Savannah River (G/G Oct. 16, 1794).	
—	Arrival at Charleston reported (C/G Nov. 27, 1794).	
—	Arrival at Charleston reported (C/G Dec. 18, 1794).	
—	Arrival at Charleston reported (C/G Jan. 19, 1795).	
—	Arrival at Charleston reported (C/G Jan. 19, 1795).	
—	"Spanish bottom" arrival reported (C/G Jan. 19, 1795).	
—	Arrival at Fort Johnson, February 9, 1795, reported (C/G Feb. 10, 1795).	
—	Arrival at Charleston November 10, 1795, one of two, reported (C/G Nov. 11, 1795).	
—		
—	Arrival at Charleston November 29, 1795, reported (C/G Nov. 30, 1795).	
—	Arrival at Charleston reported (C/G Jan. 19, 1795).	
—	Arrival at Charleston reported (C/G Feb. 9, 1795), sale of vessel reported (C/G May 20, 1795).	

Index

Vessels taken as prizes are listed on pages 127–153. Other vessels named are listed at the end of this index, pages 158–160.

Adet, Pierre (Ambassador of France), 101, 102
Aristizabal, Lieutenant General Don Gabriel (Commander, Spanish Forces in the Caribbean), 76
Ballard, Edward, 52, 53, 56, 57, 58, 59, 60, 62, 62n
Barney, Joshua, 53n
Barre, Captain Guillaume, 79n, 109
Bee, Judge Thomas (United States District Court, South Carolina), 48, 50, 51, 58, 59, 60, 70–71, 72, 73, 73n, 85n, 96
Bentley, Reverend William (diarist), 34, 44, 45, 63
Bert, Colonel (Florida Legion), 38
Blair, Judge John (United States Circuit Court, Georgia), 96
Bolchos, Captain Alexandre, 42, 43, 83
Bond, Phineas (British Consul General, Philadelphia), 79, 88n
Bouteille, Jean, 14, 17, 23, 24, 24n, 29, 30, 40, 48, 50, 51, 52, 59, 73, 74, 75, 75n, 76, 79n, 109
Branzon, Captain (of LE LASCAZAS), 28, 37, 38, 39n, 40, 42
Cambis, Admiral (French Navy), 47
Carvin, Jean Baptiste, 11–12, 14, 16, 17, 29, 40, 41, 43, 45n, 48, 50, 66n, 72, 75, 77n, 79n, 80, 81, 85, 86, 103
Castello, Captain (see *Castello* v. *Bouteille*)
Castello v. *Bouteille* (case), 48–52, 59, 73
Chaplin, Antoine, 92, 92n
Clark, George Rogers, 25
Cross & Crawley (Charleston firm), 69
Connolly, Captain (of brig GOVERNOR PINCKNEY), 94

Cunnington, Captain (Charleston Militia), 22
Cutteau, John, 92
Drayton, Stephen, 23, 25
Dupont, Victor (French Vice Consul, Charleston), 101, 102
Edwards, John, 92
d'Estaing, Admiral Charles Hector, 6
Fallon, Dr. James, 5
Fauchet, Jean Antoine Joseph (French Minister to the United States), 35, 36, 37, 38, 39, 40, 42, 47, 66, 100, 101
Ferrey, J. B. E., 100
Folger, Captain Brown (see *Folger* v. *Lecuyer*)
Folger v. *Lecuyer* (case), 18, 19
Fonspertuis, Citizen (French Vice Consul, Charleston), 41, 41n, 43, 57n, 57, 66, 82, 99, 100, 101, 102n
Fremin, Citizen (French Acting Vice Consul, St. Marys), 37
Fulton, Samuel, 101–102
Gaillard, Jean, 69, 71
Garden, Alexander, Jr., 94n (see "Rusticus")
Garriscan, Captain Henri, 79n, 81, 81n, 82, 85, 86, 86n, 109
Genêt, Edmond Charles (French Minister Plenipotentiary to the United States), 3, 6–8, 8n, 11, 12, 21, 25, 26, 27, 28, 35, 36, 36n, 37, 48, 53, 101, 109
Giles, Captain (Charleston pilot), 84, 85
Gillon, Alexander, 5, 5n, 25
Grey, General Sir Charles, 20, 31n
Hamilton, Alexander, 10, 12
Hammond, Abner, 25
Hammond, George (British Minister to the United States), 8, 12, 13n, 43, 68
Hammond, Samuel, 25
Hammond, William, 25
Hammond & Fowler (East Florida firm), 25
Henfield, Gideon, 10, 53
Hervieux, Captain Henri, 16n, 40, 49, 50, 51, 52, 76, 109
Hills, May & Woodbridge (Savannah firm), 61
Howard, Don Carlos, 102
Hugues, Victor, 63, 64, 65, 66, 84n, 86, 88–89, 104
Jansen, Joost (Master of brigantine Vrouw Christina Magdalena), 58
Jay, John, 45, 46, 99; Treaty, 97–99, 100, 101, 106
Jefferson, Thomas, 4n, 8n, 9, 13n, 31, 32
Jervis, Admiral John (later Lord St. Vincent), 20, 31n
Lang, Richard, 99–100, 102
Langlois, Joseph (Lieutenant on le Lascazas), 77n
Latalie, Captain, 79
Laveaux, General Etienne (Governor of Saint Domingue), 65, 66, 66n, 74, 75, 87, 92n
de Latre, Captain, 62
Lecuyer, Captain Jacques Louis (see *Folger* v. *Lecuyer*)

INDEX

Lory, Captain Alexandre, 79n, 87
Lowell, Judge John, 18–19
Mangourit, Michel Ange Bernard (French Consul, Charleston), 6, 21, 22, 23, 24, 25, 26, 29, 30, 35, 37, 37n, 38, 39, 40, 41, 42, 50, 99, 100
Madison James, 33
Marshall Captain (of sloop ADVICE), 22, 24
Michael, Jean, 92
Miller, Charles (British Consul, Charleston), 52n
Moissonier, Citizen (French Vice Consul, Baltimore), 12
Moodie, Benjamin (British Vice Consul, Charleston), 52 (ref. to); 55n, 60, 61, 62n, 68, 69, 70, 71n, 73, 74, 75, 79, 80, 80n, 81, 82–83, 84, 85n, 96, 97, 105
Morgan, Captain Daniel, 85
Morphy, Diogo (Spanish Consular Agent, Charleston), 100, 103
Moultrie, Governor William (of South Carolina), 25, 29, 60, 93n
Murray, Rear Admiral (British Navy), 81, 84, 104
McIntosh, John, 99
McKenney, Captain, 60
Nelson, Solomon, 53
Nepomucena de Quesada; Juan (Spanish Governor, East Florida), 100, 103 (ref. to)
North & Vesey (Charleston firm), 80
l'Ouverture, General Toussaint, 65
Pecheu, Captain, 62
Pelletier, Captain, 62
Peronne, Captain Cesar, 76, 78, 79, 80, 80n, 109
Peters, Judge Richard, 9
Pinckney, Charles Cotesworth, 99
Pinckney, General Thomas, 31
Polverel (French Commissioner, Saint Domingue), 64
Préssinet (General Laveaux's Deputy), 66, 66n
Randolph, Edmund (Attorney General of the United States), 44n
Read, Colonel Jacob, 52
Reddick, Samuel, 53, 54
Rigaud, General Andre (Commander, Department of the South, Saint Domingue), 88
Rivington Shipyard (New York), 69
Robespierre, Maxmillien, 34, 37
Rogers, Elijah, 99, 102
Ross, Captain (Master of prize ELIZABETH), 96
"Rusticus" (Alexander Garden, Jr.), 94, 94n
Rutledge, John (Chief Justice of the United States Supreme Court), 98
Sanchez, Bernardino, 27, 28
Sasportas, Abraham, 58, 69, 70, 71, 73n, 93
Sheftall Mordecai (agent), 78
Shepland, Anthony (see Chaplin, Antoine)
Shoolbred, G. (British Deputy Consul, Charleston), 30, 52n
Silvestre, Captain, 105
Sinclair, John, 52, 53, 55, 56, 57, 59, 60, 62

Sonthonax, Leger-Félicité (French Commissioner, Saint Domingue), 64
Stanley, John (President of Assembly, St. Kitts, British West Indies), 90
Sweet, Captain, 59n, 60
Talbot, William, 41, 41n, 43, 52, 53, 54, 55, 57, 59, 60, 62, 70, 78
Théric Jean François, 15n, 77n, 94, 109, 110
Trabadua, Captain Pedro, 78n, 79
Van Berkel (Resident Agent for United Netherlands), 62
Van Stabel, Rear Admiral Jean, 35, 56, 57, 58, 59
Wilson, Associate Justice James (United States Circuit Court of Appeals), 97

VESSELS OTHER THAN PRIZES

ADVICE, sloop, 22, 34
L'AIGLE, French privateer, ex-EAGLE, 103
L'AMI DE LA LIBERTÉ, French privateer schooner, 41n, 56, 57, 58, 59, 60, 62, 134–135, 136–137, 138–139, 144–145, 152–153
L'AMI DE LA POINTE-À-PITRE, French privateer schooner, 41, 42, 55, 57, 58, 59, 60, 61, 62, 70, 72, 96, 134–135, 136–137, 140–141, 148–149, 152–153 (see also FAIR PLAY)
L'ATALANTE, French privateer, 28, 28n, 128–129
BLONDE, HM frigate, 81
LA BONNE MÈRE, French privateer, 130–131
LE BRUTUS, French sloop-of-war, 35
LE BRUTUS FRANÇAIS, French privateer, ex-LE PICHEGRU, 69, 84, 85, 85n, 103, 128–129, 146–147
LE ÇA IRA, French privateer, 60n
LA CARMAGNOLE, French privateer, 12 (illustr.) 76n, 86, 104, 105, 144–145
CATHERINE, 51
LA CHARENTE, French frigate, 35
LE CITOYEN GENÊT, French privateer brig, 8, 10
CLEOPATRA, HMS, 84
LE COURIER NATIONALE, French privateer, ex-COURIER OF LIVERPOOL, 83, 84n
CYGNET, American brig, later LE GÉNÉRAL LAVEAUX, 69–72
DAEDALUS, HM frigate, 56
LE DAUPHIN, French privateer ship, ex-U.S. Continental frigate DELAWARE, 74, 75n, 83, 84n
DELAWARE, former U.S. frigate, later LE DAUPHIN, 74
EAGLE, British Letter of Marque brig, later French privateer L'AIGLE, 77, 78, 80
L'EGALITÉ, French privateer schooner, ex-L'AMI DE LA POINTE-À-PITRE, 62, 96, 134–135, 142–143, 146–147
L'EMBUSCADE, French frigate, 8n, 136–137, 140–141
FAIR MARGARET, French privateer sloop, 50
FAIR PLAY, schooner, later L'AMI DE LA POINTE-À-PITRE, 53, 54
LA FLECHA, Spanish brig, 102
FLYING FISH, New Providence privateer, 60

INDEX

LE FONSPERTUIS, French privateer, 140–141, 152–153
LE GÉNÉRAL LAVEAUX, French privateer brig, ex-CYGNET, 69, 70, 71, 72, 73, 83n, 138–139, 140–141, 142–143, 144–145, 150–151
LA GUILLOTINE, French privateer, 92n, 140–141, 148–149
HAWKE, schooner, 42, 43
HUSSAR, HM frigate, 30, 33n, 78, 19, 81
HYAENA, former British frigate, 84
L'INDUSTRIE, French privateer schooner, 11, 12–13, 17, 17n, 29, 40n, 41, 42, 48, 50, 72, 76n, 81, 128–129, 120–131, 134–135, 138–139, 148–149, 150–151
L'INTRÉPIDE, French privateer,
LE JOU JOU NATIONALE, French privateer, 140–141
LE LASCAZAS, French national vessel, schooner, 28, 29, 37, 38, 40, 41, 42, 43, 136–137
LE LEO, French privateer, 103
LA LIBERTÉ, French privateer schooner, 81n,
LITTLE JOHN (alias, see LE PETIT JEAN)
LA MÈRE MICHEL, French privateer schooner, 83, 83n, 84, 134–135, 138–139, 142–143, 152-153
LA MINERVE, French privateer, ex-MINERVA, 28, 28n, 29, 42, 128–129
LA MONTAGNE, French privateer schooner, 29, 81n, 93, 128–129, 146–147, 148–149
LA NARBONNAISE, French privateer, 76, 103, 128–129, 130–131, 132–133, 142–143, 144–145
NAUTILUS, HMS, 45n
LA PANDOUR, French privateer, 81n, 83n
LA PARISIENNE, French privateer schooner, 83, 84n, 103, 104, 132–133, 135–137, 144–145, 146–147, 148–149, 152–153
LA PATRIOTE, French privateer, 130–131
LE PETIT JEAN, French privateer, 138–139
LE PETIT PORT-DE PAIX, French privateer tender, 83n, 132–133
LA PETITE DEMOCRATE, French privateer brig, ex-LITTLE SARAH, 8, 8h
LE PORT-DE PAIX, French privateer, ex-LE VAINQUEUR DE LA BASTILLE, 74, 83n, 130–131, 132–133, 138–139, 152–153
LE PICHEGRU, French privateer brig, ex-PULASKI, 81, 82
PULASKI, brig, 69
QUEBEC, HMS, 81
LE QUI L'AUROIT PENSÉ À ÇA, French privateer, 128–129, 152–153
LE RÉPUBLICAIN, French privateer sloop, 76n, 77, 78, 80, 81, 134–135, 144–145, 148–149, 150–151, 152–153
LE ROBERT, French privateer, 29, 29n
LA RESOLUTION (see la Revolution)
LA REVOLUTION, French privateer, 137, 148–149
EL SAN ANTONIO, Spanish brig, 102
SAN JOSÉ, converted to French privateer,
LE SAN CULOTTES, French privateer, 76n, 128–129

LA SANS PAREILLE, French privateer schooner, 14–17, 17h, 29, 39n, 41, 42, 43, 48, 50, 75, 128–129, 130–131, 134–135, 136–137, 138–139, 140–141, 144–145, 148–149, 150–151

SCORPION, HM sloop-of-war, 78, 81

LA SIGNORIA, 76

SIR CHARLES GREY, British privateeer ship, 85

LA TENDRE MÈRE, French privateer, 140–141

TERPSICHORE, HM frigate, 81

THETIS, HM frigate, 81, 82

LE VAINQUER DE LA BASTILLE, French privateer, 15, 130–131

LE VENGEUR, French privateer, 86, 103, 104, 138–139, 144–145, 146–147, 152–153

LE VENGEUR DE RISQUE-TOUT (see LE VENGEUR)

LE VENGEUR DE SANS CULOTTES (see LE VENGEUR)

LE VOLCAN, French privateer, ex-LE PORT-DE-PAIX, 132–133

LE VAN STABEL, French privateer, 47n